# STATISTICS, SCIENCE AND PUBLIC POLICY

### VIII. SCIENCE, ETHICS AND THE LAW

# STATISTICS, SCIENCE AND PUBLIC POLICY

## VIII. SCIENCE, ETHICS AND THE LAW

Proceedings of the Conference on
Statistics, Science and Public Policy
held at Herstmonceux Castle, Hailsham, U.K.
April 23-26, 2003

A.M. HERZBERG *and* R.W. OLDFORD *Editors*

**National Library of Canada Cataloguing in Publication**

Conference on Statistics, Science and Public Policy (8th : 2004 :
Hailsham, England)
    Statistics, science and public policy VIII : science, ethics and the law :
proceedings of the Conference on Statistics, Science and Public Policy held at
Herstmonceux Castle, Hailsham, U.K., April 23-26, 2003 / A.M. Herzberg and
R.W. Oldford, editors.

    Includes bibliographical references.
ISBN 1-55339-067-9

    1. Science—Moral and ethical aspects—Congresses. 2. Science and law—
Congresses. I. Herzberg, A. M. II. Oldford, R. W., 1954-     III. Title.

Q175.35.C65 2004      174'.95      C2004-900921-4

Cover by Graphic Design: Peter Dorn

Photograph of Herstmonceux Castle courtesy of Dee Padfield

# Table of Contents

# Foreword

These proceedings summarize the sessions of the conference on Statistics, Science and Public Policy, with the theme Science, Ethics and the Law, which was held at Herstmonceux Castle in the United Kingdom, April 23–26, 2003. This was the eighth conference in the series Statistics, Science and Public Policy.

Since the conference was aimed at promoting dialogue, participants who made presentations were free to choose their own format. Some gave formal papers, others were more informal, and one or two spoke extemporaneously, adjusting their remarks in light of the discussions. The papers and speeches have been edited or summarized for publication by the authors and editors.

A.M. Herzberg
R.W. Oldford
February 2004

# Acknowledgements

The conference would not have taken place without the advice and help of many: D.F. Andrews, P. Calamai, D.R. Cox, H.B. Dinsdale, B. Farbey, D.J. Hand, K.W. James, I. Krupka and P. Milliken. These, along with many others, provided welcome advice. A. Morgan, J. Whittle and J. Zakos, as always, provided valuable assistance and timely encouragement.

Support from Queen's University came through the kind offices of the Vice-Principals, Advancement and Research. This included funding as well as the help of H. Bennett.

The financial and in-kind contributions of the following are appreciated: Berry Brothers and Rudd, Ltd.; Camera Kingston; Campus Bookstore, Queen's University; the Canada Foundation for Innovation; Environment Canada; Galerie d'Art Vincent, Château Laurier, Ottawa; National Research Council of Canada; Natural Resources Canada; Natural Sciences and Engineering Research Council of Canada; and many anonymous donors.

The excellent work of a remarkable set of individuals is gratefully acknowledged: the editorial expertise of M. Banting and S. Fraser; the production work of M. Howes and V. Jarus of the Publications Unit of the School of Policy Studies, Queen's University; and P. Dorn's continuing design work for the conference, including the covers of these proceedings.

Mr. M. Cappe, Canadian High Commissioner to the United Kingdom, hosted the welcoming reception and opened the conference.

Mr. Gerald Finley, the well-known Canadian baritone, and Julius Drake, the accomplished British pianist, gave a recital in the ballroom of Herstmonceux Castle on the second evening, thus furnishing a memorable musical ambience.

# Contributors

W.B. Allen, Michigan State University

E.B. Andersen, University of Copenhagen

J.C. Bailar III, University of Chicago

F.H. Berkshire, Imperial College of Science, Technology and Medicine

P. Calamai, *Toronto Star*

V.M. Del Buono, British Council, Nigeria

H.B. Dinsdale, Kingston General Hospital and Queen's University

B. Farbey, University College London

D.J. Hand, Imperial College of Science, Technology and Medicine

R.T. Haworth, Natural Resources Canada

A.M. Herzberg, Queen's University

R.J. Howard, Harvard University/Key3 Media

D.H. Irvine, Picker Institute, Europe

T. Jefferson, Cochrane Vaccines Field

P. Kavanagh, Canadian Broadcasting Corporation

J.S.C. McKee, University of Manitoba

R.H. McKercher, McKercher, McKercher and Whitmore, Saskatoon

M.S. McQuigge, Owen Sound, Canada

A.F. Merry, University of Auckland

R.W. Oldford, University of Waterloo

P. Park, Discovery Channel, Canada

G.H. Reynolds, Centers for Disease Control and Prevention

J.M. Spence, Superior Court of Justice of Ontario

L. Wolpert, University College London

# PART I

INTRODUCTION

CHAPTER 1

# Science, Ethics and the Law: The Discussion

## A.M. Herzberg

Each of the words — science, ethics, law — in the title may be considered individually and in pairs to determine their interactions. Is there a difference between ethics and morality? Should identity cards be required of every individual in every country? Are they becoming necessary because of the current worries about terrorism? Would they be effective? What are the pros and cons of stem-cell research and the pitfalls of genetic profiling? Is it ethical to show pictures of the war on television? Does showing pictures of prisoners-of-war violate the Geneva Convention? All of these issues have become part of our lives today. All of these questions will be considered over the course of this volume.

At the first conference on Statistics, Science and Public Policy in 1996, mad cow disease (BSE, bovine spongiform encephalitis) had just come to the fore, and it was discussed then, and in later conferences, how badly its appearance had been handled by the politicians in the United Kingdom and of the scientific, medical and political implications of the disease. The participants at the conference worried about the closing of research establishments in Canada and the continuing problems of, among others, fluoride in water and electromagnetic fields. In 2001, it was the terrible situation of foot and mouth disease. One could not walk on the country paths. At the same time, we were concerned about *E.coli* outbreaks. In 2002, terrorism and health and the environment were major issues. In 2003, it was the scarcity of water, the continued fear of terrorism, bioterrorism and cyberterrorism, and war and the serious increase in multi-drug resistant diseases and most recently SARS (severe acute respiratory syndrome). Why have these crises appeared and not always been dealt with in the most expedious way?

## ETHICS AND EDUCATION

John Polanyi has said:

We have struggled for a long time to come to terms with the fact that our universities serve the public interest best when free of government inter-ference in academic affairs. We have now to come to terms with the fact that these same institutions should, in everyone's interest, be substantially free from the influence as to what is taught or thought, even by such an interested party as industry. Compromise will be necessary, but the funda-mental principle is sound (Polanyi, 2002, p. A19).

Two editorials by Donald Kennedy, editor-in-chief of *Science* and past president of Stanford University, have brought a number of im-portant issues to the fore. In his editorial of January 31, 2003 titled "An Epidemic of Politics", he begins by saying:

Americans have come to accept the role of politics in the appointment of certain kinds of public officials. Few of us are surprised, though some may be disappointed, when a federal judgeship is awarded because the candi-date passes a litmus test of loyalty to some principle important to the president's party. Scientific appointments, however, should rest on more objective criteria of training, ability, and performance — at least, that's what this community has always believed (Kennedy, 2003*a,* p. 625).

He follows with two examples:

A nominee for the National Institutes of Health Muscular Dystrophy Research Coordinating Committee is vetted by a staffer from the Office of White House Liaison, Health and Human Services. After being asked about her views on various Bush administration policies, none of them related to the work of the committee, she is asked whether she supports the presi-dent's embryonic stem cell policy.

A distinguished professor of psychiatry and psychology receives a call from the White House about his nomination to serve on the National Council on Drug Abuse. His interviewer declares that he must vet him to "deter-mine whether he held any views that might be embarrassing to the president." A series of questions follows, into which the interviewer interpolates a running score, *viz.*: "You're two for three; the president opposes needle exchange on moral grounds regardless of the outcome." He then asks whether the candidate had voted for Bush, and on being informed that he had not, asked: "Why didn't you support the president?" (ibid.).

Political loyalty should not come into the appointment of members of such committees nor should one be asked to reveal one's political affiliation. In a democracy each person has an independent say and the right to privacy. Are we getting away from democracy and liberty? This is a serious question at the present time. Kennedy goes on to say that:

> This stuff would be prime material for a ... comedy, ... but it really isn't funny. The purpose of advisory committees is to provide balanced, thoughtful advice to the policy process; it is better not to put the policy up front.... deciding which research projects to support has always been a matter for objective peer review. Political preferences are for the pork barrel (ibid.).

In the same vein in relation to science, has integrity disappeared? Has peer review become "you scratch my back and I'll scratch yours"? This seems prevalent in many places in society, not just in science. Are the proper procedures of, for example, peer review being followed irrespective of the results?

In another editorial "Inspection Science" on February 28, 2003, Kennedy denounces the impending war in Iraq and discusses the search for evidence of weapons of mass destruction. He notes that Rolf Ekeus, chairman of the United Nations Monitory, Verification and Inspection Commission (UNMOVIC), has said that the most helpful technique in their work is "analysis".

> [Ekeus] explained that what made the largest difference for inspectors was the capacity to gather and interpret large amounts of intelligence and other data from various sources, and then separate the useful signals from the noise.... [This] requires the capacity to gather data in various ways, not all of which have been available to UNMOVIC until quite recently. It requires well-trained, thoughtful analysts, who are critical components of the inspection regime. Above all, it requires time. Are we prepared to wage war when the experiment has barely started? (Kennedy, 2003*b*, p. 1281).

Here the discipline of statistics and the statistician have made their mark and this demonstrates why "statistics" is an essential part of the conference title.

## ETHICS AND THE LAW

We now have war without a United Nations resolution. Has the law of nations been broken? Jean Chrétien, then Prime Minister of Canada, felt that war without a United Nations resolution would be wrong. Did George Bush and Tony Blair break international law? Could they be considered to be war criminals? Did Bush and Blair proceed in spite of the lack of agreement within the United Nations because of the old adages: "Convince a man against his will, he's of the same opinion still." and "Don't confuse me with facts my mind's made up."

In his March 28, 2003 editorial, Donald Kennedy says that for "the task of reconstruction" after the war "whatever nations and agencies join in, then the work will need the full arsenal of science and technology: to repair infrastructure, to deliver aid to civilians, to protect the public health, and to start rebuilding a national economy" and he ends by saying that "whatever the US president thinks of the UN, it is hard to identify another institution that can serve as the 'indispensable partner'" (Kennedy, 2003c, p. 1945).

What is natural justice and what is the law or the workings of the law? Is natural justice the law that is not written down — does it include ethics or is it merely the right to be heard? Is natural justice the belief that power itself may be evil or that punishment should fit the crime? Could the burning of witches be considered "natural justice", or was it a travesty against natural justice? Does natural justice depend on the times?

Is law the embodiment of ethics which then later becomes public policy?

What is the relationship between ethics and virtue? Do their meanings overlap? Jacob Bronowski wrote that:

> By the worldly standards of public life, all scholars in their work are oddly virtuous. They do not make wild claims, they do not chant, they do not try to persuade at any cost, they appeal neither to prejudice nor to authority, they are often frank about their ignorance, their disputes are fairly decorous, they do not confuse what is being argued with race, politics, sex or age, they listen patiently to the young and to the old who both know everything. These are the general virtues of scholarship, and they are peculiarly the virtues of science (Bronowski, 1961, p. 67).

In 1971, Jacob Bronowski anticipated Donald Kennedy when he said that:

No science is immune to the infection of politics and the corruption of power.... The time has come to consider how we might bring about a separation as complete as possible, between Science and Government in all countries. I call this the *disestablishment of science,* in the same sense in which the churches have been disestablished and have become independent of the state (Bronowski 1971, p. 15).

In this article, Bronowski claims that when scientists become members of government committees they often become "prisoner[s] of the procedures by which governments everywhere are told only what they want to hear, and tell the public only what they want to have it believe" (ibid., p. 13).

In 1939, Dr. Leo Szilard proposed that physicists should make a voluntary agreement not to publish any new findings on the fission of uranium because of its potential for destruction. Bronowski commented that:

Far-sighted as Leo Szilard was, it is hard to believe that the events he feared could have been stopped even if the scientists he canvassed had accepted his invitation to silence. The embargo on publication that he tried to improvise was [crudely unrealistic], in a field in which discoveries were being made so [rapidly] and their implications were [both] clear and ... grave. At best, Szilard's scheme could have been [only a] stop-gap with which he might [have hoped] to buy a little time (Bronowski, 1971, p. 9).

## ETHICS AND BUSINESS

In an article in the *Financial Times* (2002), titled "Aristotle Was Right" with the subtitle "He said there are some jobs where virtue is impossible", the question is: Are there business leaders of virtue? Is it becoming harder to find those with a spotless past? Perhaps not, but if so, can capitalism flourish on virtue?

Successful businesses are created by risk-takers who survive by exploiting opportunities against cut-throat competition — usually motivated by hope of big rewards.

Their behaviour may be morally questionable on occasion and, if allowed to run to extremes, would [itself] undermine the [healthy] operation of capitalism (*Financial Times*, 2002).

Perhaps this is what Edward Heath called "the unacceptable face of capitalism".

It is the state's job to curb excesses through law and regulation (where a repentant poacher is often the most effective gamekeeper). Better the hard work of creating the right business environment than the endless search for the Holy Grail of a saintly tycoon (ibid.).

There is a decline in what is known as the work ethic and a laxness in attitudes. The public calls out for more government services, yet also wants tax cuts. How many have never participated in the black market or underground economy?

Is it ethical to provide free education but not necessarily free medicine? In 1954, Tommy Douglas, leader of the Canadian Commonwealth Federation (CCF), said in the Saskatchewan Legislative Assembly "I made a pledge to myself that some day, if I ever had anything to do with it, people would be able to get health services just as they are able to get educational services, as an inalienable right of being a citizen." Eight years later he made it happen.

## CONCLUSION

Can we influence governments? If we do not act, nothing will happen and governments can carry on, believing that the public does not really care.

Ones does not want to have the situation described by Sir Thomas Browne (1605–1682) "A man may be in as just possession of truth as of a city, and yet be forced to surrender."

If only the real world were like crime stories where law and order are certain to triumph in the end.

## REFERENCES

Bronowski, J. (1961), *Science and Human Values*. London: Hutchinson.
_____ (1971), "The Disestablishment of Science", *Encounter* 35(1):8-16.
*Financial Times* (2002), "Aristotle Was Right", November 30/December 1.
Kennedy, D. (2003a), "An Epidemic of Politics", (Editorial) *Science* 299:625.
_____(2003b), "Inspection Science", (Editorial) *Science* 299:1281.
_____(2003c), "Science and the War", (Editorial). *Science* 299:1945.
Polanyi, J.C. (2002), "The Act of Discovery", *Ottawa Citizen*, November 26, p. A19.

CHAPTER 2

# The Law, Science and Ethics

M.S. McQuigge

## INTRODUCTION

The theme for the 2003 conference on Statistics, Science and Public Policy is science, ethics and the law. Some definitions of the law include "the law specifically refers to the rules laid down by the sovereign power in a nation", "a rule of conduct, recognized by custom or decreed by formal enactment, considered by a community, nation, or other authoritatively constituted group as binding upon its members" (Funk and Wagnell's *Standard College Dictionary*, Canadian Edition).

Law and lawyers appear frequently in *Bartlett's Familiar Quotations*:

The Law is the true embodiment
Of everything that's excellent
It has no kind of fault or flaw
And I, my Lords embody the law. (William S. Gilbert)

In law, what plea so tainted and corrupt
But being seasoned with a gracious voice
Obscures the show of evil. (William Shakespeare)

The first thing we do, let's kill all the lawyers. (William Shakespeare)

The law is the last result of human wisdom acting upon experience for the benefit of the public. (Samuel Johnson)

The Law, wherein, as in a magic mirror, we see reflected not only our own lives, but the lives of all men that have been! When we think on this majestic theme, my eyes dazzle. (Oliver Wendell Holmes)

As scientists and individuals, that is probably how we all view the law, sometimes with disdain, and sometimes with a feeling that the law protects us and provides order in the face of chaos.

I shall look at aspects of this theme through my experience as a clinical physician and a former medical officer of health, but still as one who is very interested in public health.

## THE LAW AS A FAILURE OF SOCIETY AND SCIENTIFIC COMMUNICATION

If everyone were honest and ethical, the notion is that one would not need laws. Having a law means, in part, a failure to convince people that behaving in a certain manner is the correct and obvious thing to do. In the earlier part of this century, public health inspectors acted like police. If a mattress were infected with lice, inspectors dragged it out onto the lawn and set it on fire — no question that the neighbours formed a quick opinion of you! Today's public health officials would rather educate the public that a certain course of action is correct rather than use the laws to force compliance. For the most part this has led to better compliance, but there have been recent events that have challenged that approach (McQuigge, 2002*a*).

Before the Walkerton water disaster, compliance in ensuring safe drinking water was done voluntarily through the *Ontario Drinking Water Guidelines* (McQuigge, 2002*c*). The guidelines had no force in law. Within three months of the Walkerton disaster, the *Ontario Safe Drinking Water Act* was proclaimed and the guidelines were changed to legal regulations. Penalties were ascribed to those who failed to obey the regulations. Has this approach worked better? Perhaps, but there are plenty of incidences where penalties continue to be meted out to those in violation of the regulations. Legal threat does not necessarily alter behaviour.

What is the best course of action? Perhaps the best approach is to continue to persuade and educate the public as to the wisdom of good public health interventions, with the laws used as a back-up in the event that non-compliance is a threat to society's health (McQuigge, 2000). The recent SARS (severe acute respiratory syndrome) outbreak in Toronto highlights this approach: people who were in contact with SARS cases were asked to voluntarily quarantine themselves.[1] Most did, but a handful of people who did not were forcibly confined to hospital for observation. There was some talk of using electronic locator bracelets to track the whereabouts of SARS contacts. There are serious concerns about civil liberties during an emergency such as this.

It is clear that in the case of SARS, laws will not contain the disease. Rather, international co-operation in identifying and containing the disease, plus tests quickly pinpointing its biological cause, providing a quick method of testing those who are ill and providing new treatment methods are the things that will turn the tide. As China will learn the hard way, it is better to be open and forthcoming about a new epidemic and to seek the co-operation and help of other nations as well as the World Health Organization.

There is a place for health laws when it comes to those who are too young to make informed decisions. The tobacco laws are a good example: banning the sale of tobacco products to minors makes good sense and sends a message to the youth that adults are concerned about their future health.

Science at its best would be so effective at communication that where science has an impact on the health and safety of people, individuals will see the rationale of adjusting their behaviour and then laws would be unnecessary. For some, laws are a failure of science to communicate effectively.

## DOES THE LAW REFLECT GOOD SCIENCE?

Two years have passed since the Walkerton inquiry and some of the lawyers involved have made comments publicly. One was that the inquiry might have been futile in that its focus seemed to be to take in just the edges. The statement was that the inquiry offered a chance for everyone to take a shot at everyone else, and, in the process, seed doubts about the "good guys" and make the "bad guys" look less bad. The notion is that the inquiry could have stopped at the point of the early investigative report, which was monetarily cheaper and straightforward, and that little was really added by an enlarged inquiry.

My own view is that the process served as a means of healing a community badly ravaged by an epidemic (McQuigge, 2002*b*). The inquiry also provided an excellent opportunity for scientists to suggest ways of preventing such a disaster in the future. The recommendations from the commissioner of the inquiry were thoughtful and were based on scientific evidence. The learning experience has involved observing the political process of bringing, or not bringing, these recommendations into law.

I asked one lawyer to reflect on the aftermath of the Walkerton disaster and he said that from a lawyer's perspective, it was over and he was on to the next case. Only lawyers involved in legal policy-making would be interested in reflecting on the past.

## THE LAW AS POLITICS

It is said that the law is the end result of politics and that politics is the "art of the possible". This can mean that when science suggests the correct approach to a problem, the law, because of politics, may choose to ignore the science or shape the response in a way that is unsatisfactory to scientists.

I believe that there are a number of trends that one should be concerned about. Society is producing more and more lawyers. Many politicians in Canada are lawyers and this in a time when some people believe that lawyers are not well respected. In Japan, fifty years ago there were less than a thousand lawyers in the whole country. Business deals were sealed by a handshake (perhaps because one's word was a trust and also that going back on your word could result in things being settled by violent means). Now Japanese business deals involve lawyers. Is this trend toward increasing legalization driven by the lawyers or by a society that does not trust anymore?

Few scientists are politicians; therefore, little scientific voice is brought to political decisions unless scientists are expressly asked to give an opinion, as consultants on working groups or as invited participants at the discussion level. Scientific participation is by invitation rather than being a given part of the process.

There is an essay in *Essays in the History of Canadian Law* that reviews Ontario Water Quality, Public Health, and the Law from 1880 to 1930 (Benidickson, 1999). The essay might just as well have included up to the present. What the essay concludes is that political, agricultural and business interests have managed to stall good laws designed to ensure safe drinking water. The Ontario government just put off enacting a new nutrient management law *until 2008 at the earliest.*

## WHOSE LAW?

The law reflects politics and the ethics of the day. There are some individuals who believe that evolution is just a theory. Ethics and the law are often at odds, stealing a loaf of bread in some countries can lead to the loss of a hand!

In Canada there is a movement among Aboriginal people to have some laws apply to justice among native peoples only. In Saskatchewan, there is a disproportionate number of native people in the jails and the recidivism rate is high. Mark Lachman views this as a failure of opportunity (Lachman, 2003). The law is perceived differently in each culture and it may be time to investigate the different forms of justice and the law in order to find the most effective.

## The Blame Society

This winter, in Owen Sound, an elderly woman was found frozen to death in her house. The newspaper article discussed how her death could have been prevented. Neighbours commented that the woman was a loner and had rebuffed all attempts at conversation, friendliness or aid. In other words, the person had alienated herself from her community to the point where her neighbours did not talk to her or check up on her. And yet, one neighbour was quoted as saying "I am so confused about her death, I don't know who to blame!"

Without belabouring this point, our society no longer seems to accept that there are natural mistakes or moments of forgetfulness, and that the phrase "to err is human" is a reality. Rather, present society expects that there should always be a perfect outcome. If not, a lawyer should be hired, someone should be hauled into court and blame apportioned. There needs to be a place to bring people to justice who have truly harmed others through criminal acts or negligence, but society seems out of balance on this (Garrett, 2000).

This attitude has had a profound effect on science and particularly, on medicine. Physician insurance rates have risen to the point where the president of the United States recently felt compelled to comment. The worry of being sued has seen many physicians leave the profession early. In Canada, a decade ago, 33 per cent of new medical graduates entered general practice. It was close to 90 per cent thirty years ago. In 2003, only 24 per cent chose general practice; reasons were given as the difficulty of keeping up with all new aspects of medicine and the probability of being sued. And many of those who stay in practice often order many unnecessary and costly tests in order to protect themselves. This has meant that physicians' behaviour is less governed by science and more by the threat of legal action. This is not a good thing for society and not a good thing for patient care.

Standards of care in medicine are quickly becoming legally binding on physicians. Standards are derived from evidence-based medicine:

research that looks critically at what does and does not work, often involving statistical and epidemiological research. This is a good process and reflects the term "Decision Science" used by C.C. Heyde in 2000 (Heyde, 2001). However, the process is not perfect, nor does it always reflect the complexity of care that needs flexibility. In other words, standards are black and white, whereas the practice of medicine is sometimes not so clear. Medical students are expected to be well-versed in the standards of care in order to pass exams. Do not misunderstand me, standards of care are one of the best developments in the practice of medicine. However, the older physician part of me has seen some standards of care change radically over the years. For example, hormone replacement therapy in women was supposed to protect women from heart disease and it has now been found to actually increase the risk of heart disease and stroke. My point is that standards of care are an evolving science and do not always represent the final word.

## The Scared Society

The political process of determining the law has already had a real impact on science. Major recent developments such as cloning, genetically modified foods and the unraveling of the human genome have made society nervous. Society is more skeptical and scared of the ethics of scientists and the difficulty of predicting the impact of these developments. As a result, laws have been considered that would ban further cloning research and the marketing of genetically modified foods. Patent laws have been used to own parts of the human genetic code.

This is an area where science has progressed beyond society's ability to absorb and understand such rapid and profound changes. The instinct is to say, "let's pause, look at the consequences and then decide whether and how to proceed". We need to understand this natural anxiety and reaction, and be part of the process of resolving these issues to everyone's satisfaction.

## CONCLUSION

Science, ethics and the law are often uncomfortable with each other. Lack of good communication from scientists can result in bad law, bad politics, a society that does not trust, and a society that looks for legal solutions when it would be better served by good dialogue.

One thing seems reasonably certain: when science, ethics and the law do converge, one has the makings of a just and fair society.

## NOTE

1. At the time of this presentation (April 23, 2003), the World Health Organization had issued a travel advisory against travelling to Toronto.

## REFERENCES

Benidickson, J. (1999), "Ontario Water Quality, Public Health, and the Law, 1880-1930", in *Essays in the History of Canadian Law*, ed. C.B. Baker and J. Phillips. Toronto: The Osgoode Society for Canadian Legal History, pp. 115-141.

Garrett, L. (2000), *The Betrayal of Trust*. New York: Hyperion.

Heyde, C.C. (2001), "The Changing Scene for Higher Education in Science: A View from the Statistical Profession", in *Statistics, Science and Public Policy V. Society, Science and Education*, ed. A.M. Herzberg and I. Krupka. Kingston, ON: Queen's University, pp. 13-23.

Lachman, M. (2003), "Environment and Health: The Aboriginal Experience in Canada", in *Statistics, Science and Public Policy VII. Environment, Health and Globalization*, ed. A.M. Herzberg and R.W. Oldford. Kingston, ON: Queen's University, pp. 123-126.

McQuigge, M. (2000), "Diseases: New and Emerging", *The Canadian Journal of Continuing Medical Education* (April):133-150.

_____ (2002*a*), "Another Sign of the Demise of Environmental Protection and Public Health in Developed Countries", in *Statistics, Science and Public Policy VI. Science and Responsibility*, ed. A.M. Herzberg and R.W. Oldford. Kingston, ON: Queen's University, pp. 253-257.

_____ (2002*b*), "The Walkerton Disaster and Family Physicians", *Canadian Family Physician* (October):1596-1597.

_____ (2002*c*), "Water: A Clear and Present Danger", *The Canadian Journal of Public Health* 93(1):10-11.

# PART II

## SCIENCE IN THE COURTS

CHAPTER 3

# The Laws of Science and the Rule of Law

W.B. Allen

Louise Robbins died in 1987. Though a distinguished anthropologist, the North Carolina professor's death was an event mainly unnoticed save by the community of expert witnesses and associated prosecuting and defence attorneys with whom she had collaborated in more than a score of United States and Canadian legal cases for better than a decade. And for a decade following her death, they continued to debate Louise Robbins' science. For, among other things, this field anthropologist boasted an exact knowledge of identifying indicia from footprints and even boot prints. On one expedition to Tanzania she revealed the hidden text of a 3.5 million year-old fossilized print: a five-and-one-half months pregnant woman. Such forensic exactitude was not to be kept out of court, where countless suspects constantly await conviction or exoneration upon a definitive showing of relevant facts.

While courts are often thought of as law forums, they are far more dramatically triers of fact: for the application of law is utterly dependent upon an authoritative reading of the facts. The question is: Who knows the facts? Scientists like to imagine that this is our exclusive domain, for indeed the laws of science were established precisely to determine knowledge of facts. Moreover, the courts have been all too willing to concede our claim, up to a point. That critical point — judgement point, deriving from its Greek source, *krinō*— is the determination of just who is a scientist. For a long time we have been stuck between the impracticality, if not impossibility, of defending the autonomy of the law if we insist that scientists alone may speak with authority about science, on the one hand, and the grave and enormous potential danger to human inquiry if it is left to the law to determine authoritatively what constitutes science. Informed observers are aware of the postures this dilemma has assumed in debates about abortion and cloning. I do not address those issues, preferring instead to demonstrate from issues that are not life-and-death just how imposing this dilemma has become.

The Louise Robbins case is particularly of interest precisely because her career took aim squarely at the 1923 U.S. "Frye Rule", which set forth legal steps for answering this question, founded upon the court's accommodating itself to scientific authentication of science.[1] The central and most important of the Frye Rules was the bar against scientific eccentricity, that is, evidence would be admissible only if it "is sufficiently established to have gained general acceptance in the particular field to which it belongs". This pre-Popperian notion of falsifiability was content to rely on consensus in the scientific community to reject a so-called "deception test" (pre-cursor to the lie detector) as what is now called "junk science".

It would be appropriate for the skeptic to insist that I have overdrawn the dilemma, since a legal determination of what is *admissible* as science is not grammatically the same thing as determining what science is. I will show, however, that this slippery slope is perceivable only after one has slid down it.

Louise Robbins slipped through the Frye Rule, sending at least a dozen people to prison and one to death row, despite the fact that no one ever replicated her findings and that she could never articulate a systematic foundation of her putative knowledge. Indeed, she became a feet-reading celebrity in courtrooms, practising a science where no one else knew one to exist. Did she, as one critic belatedly remarked, "make a mockery out of the criminal justice system?" (Hansen, 1993, p. 64).

Some would say that the U.S. Congress, and not the court, opened the door to a claim of science in a case where there was never a test, no peer-reviewed publication, and no corroborative research. In 1978, Congress passed legislation, "Federal Rules of Evidence," that made no reference to *Frye's* standard of "general acceptance in the field". Robbins, however, did her work prior to a definitive 1993 Supreme Court ruling on the new legislation,[2] and in a context in which most courts still practised Frye Rules. The problem, ultimately, was not a changed rule but an inherent difficulty.

This difficulty shows up in many ways contemporaneous with Robbins's infamous work, but ultimately in one question contemporaneous both with *Frye* and Robbins. In 1995, summary judgement was granted in favour of GTE Mobilnet in a lawsuit that claimed a cellphone caused the growth of a brain tumor, the court having declared the plaintiff's argument "a kind of ... junk science".[3] In 1996 the U.S. District Court for the District of Columbia, forcing the hands of the Food and Drug Administration and the Federal Trade Commission, required restaurants to justify health and nutrition claims in food/menu labelling just as food packagers do under the *Nutrition Labeling and Education Act* (*Legal Backgrounder*, 1996). And in 2002, one Todd Brown defended his Master's thesis, entitled "The Morphology of Calcium Carbonate: Factors Affecting Crystal Shape", against a University of California decision refusing to award the degree because the thesis contained a "dis-acknowledgements" section in which Brown wrote "F...k you" to university administrators and California's Governor Davis (McAvee, 2002, p. A4). Because his case was rejected at every judicial level prior to the U.S. Supreme Court, Mr. Brown announced a reconsideration of his career choice, abandoning science for the law! As recently as 1999 a New Jersey school board had to decide, subject to court review, whether a high school physics teacher could be removed because of searching pornography sites on the Internet while conducting physics instruction (*National Law Journal*, 1999, p. A23).

The foregoing cases may seem quirky and unproblematic, compared with Louise Robbins. But consider one further case, formally similar to the New Jersey case. Roger De Hart is a science teacher in the State of Washington. In 1999 De Hart was ordered to stop including instruction in "intelligent design" in his high school biology class. He and his school district were challenged by the American Civil Liberties Union because De Hart had for ten or twelve years consistently paired the teaching of evolution with the teaching of "intelligent design" (Gibeaut, 1999, p. 50). Although he religiously avoided mention of God, Creation, or religion, his effort was viewed as part of a large, national movement to bring creationism into the school curriculum. Opponents (often scientists) saw it as pushing anti-science, and worse, religion, in the face of a definitive 1987 Supreme Court ruling.[4]

It is surpassingly ironic that debates about the role of science in the courts, in the United States at least, continue to revolve around issues once settled in the 1923–24 era, and matters no less non-controversial than controversial.

The Frye Rule of 1923 never generated the dramas sustained by the so-called "Scopes Monkey Trial",[5] yet each addressed the issue of science in the courts. At the same time as one court, the *Frye* court, appealed to scientific consensus as decisive, the other court — the *Scopes* court — arrogated the right and power to declare what was and was not science. I submit that the *Scopes* result was a necessary consequence of the *Frye* orientation.

This does not occur merely because scientists, like all others, organize around perceived opportunities to exploit their interests. Some proposed reforms of the past twenty years would have addressed these dilemmas by establishing science courts, independent of law courts, naïvely imagining that official scientists who had decided a question one way, would not have exerted every possible influence, licit and illicit, ethical and unethical, to assure that a subsequent legal decision would have agreed with them. But the tendency of scientists, like everyone else, to be politicians first, is not responsible for the dynamic between *Frye* and *Scopes*; — that is, from scientific *laissez-faire* to "somebody's got to judge".

The easy way to explain this phenomenon would be to point out the exaggeration of the laws of science, which can never be completely compatible with legal thinking that must presume stable order even when it knowingly does not favour it. The truer account, though, has to do with the direct relationship of science and law. Science is a necessary tool of law. Without science the law could not perpetuate the myth of sufficiency of judgement. Science is nothing less than the legal community's defence against the jury, which is to say, uninstructed opinion. Once that relationship became clear to legal minds, despite *Frye's* attempt at "live and let live" accommodation, there was no choice but for law to begin to set the boundaries of science, or to avoid creating new Galilean martyrs by making would-be Galileo's their own policemen. The formula in *Frye*, rendered practically, is "you scientists get together and keep the crackpots out of our hair, and we, in turn, will assure that you are not disturbed by idle tomfoolery". That is the sense in which *Scopes* is naturally paired with *Frye*.

One sees this dynamic at work not immediately in *Scopes* but in the pair of 1980s' cases that revisited *Scopes*. (It is useful to remember that *Scopes* did not reach the United States Supreme Court). It is only necessary to bear in mind that these decisions were being rendered shortly after the "Federal Rules of Evidence" were revised (and before the Supreme Court interpreted them to open the door to novel science claims), and while truly difficult scientific questions in the life sciences and in the computer software industry were bubbling to the forefront. In short, courts were asked to police science in the life sciences and computer software areas, at the same time as it had elected anew to defend science against fundamentalism in the form of creationism. The relationship was perfectly reciprocal, and an ideal pairing. And the result defines now, and doubtless for a long time to come, the role of science in the courts.

To understand this requires but a brief summary of the 1980s' cases and related materials. In 1981, the State of Arkansas established *Public Act 590*, commanding that "public schools within this State shall give balanced treatment to creation-science and to evolution-science". This act was challenged as unconstitutional in Federal District Court by Reverend Bill McLean and others, on the grounds that it violates the First Amendment protection against an establishment of religion, that it violated a right to academic freedom and that it suffered from vagueness incompatible with due process protections in the U.S. Constitution.[6] The District Court ruled against the state and for McLean on the basis of an "evaluation" of the "scientific merit" of creation-science. The court held that the methods, practices and premises of this so-called science fell squarely outside the methods, practices and premises of "the scientific community" and, moreover, could only be understood as a religious claim based on the *Bible*. The act "lacks legitimate educational value because 'creation science' as defined in [the Act] is simply not science ... Science is what is accepted by the scientific community and is 'what scientists do'". And what is science? "(i) It is guided by natural law; (ii) It has to be explanatory by reference to natural law; (iii) It is testable against the empirical world; (iv) Its conclusions are tentative, i.e., are not necessarily the final word; and (v) It is falsifiable".[7] We could greatly expatiate on the confusion of "laws of nature" with "natural law" and the notion of a world "empirical", but the present task forces us to treat such claims as unproblematic. Thus, while it is evident that the court relied upon orthodox opinions concerning the nature of science, what is of moment is the use of those opinions to construct an authoritative, legally binding definition of science, which may be applied to exclude or include specific scientific claims or practices based on enforceable legal determination.

In such light, the contemporary debates on issues such as stem-cell research or cloning take on an entirely different hue. To insist upon the independence or autonomy of science at the same time as relying upon the authority of the state to give force to scientific consensus may represent mutually exclusive, contradictory alternatives. This prospect loomed large in the court's discussion of the "comet seeding theory" of the origins of life on earth by "Dr. Wickramasinghe". While this eccentric, outlying theory "has not received general acceptance within the scientific community, he has, at least, used scientific methodology to produce a theory of origins which meets the *essential characteristics* of science".[8] In other words, however the court derives its notion of science, it is free to apply the notion based on its own interpretation of any particular scientific claim.

We question the discussion of the role of legal authority in defining science, when the activity clearly arises as a result of legislative enactments. To remove the courts from such roles does not imply removing the state from attempts to infringe upon the autonomy of science. And many observers would prefer the deliberative forum of a court to the potential rule of general public opinion, likely to influence a legislature. To pose the question that way, however, fails to enlarge the option for courts to embrace a self-denying ordinance, "it is not our job to say what science is", upon which basis it may still restrain legislative excesses, "the meaning of science may not be legislated". On the latter path political restraints upon science will extend no further than public funding or non-funding of specific scientific practices would necessarily imply. That there might be danger in the nexus between politics and science all but the hopelessly naïve must concede. But the withdrawal of a grant does not produce a Galilean martyr.

The fullest implication of *McLean* was made manifest in a 1987 case decided by the U.S. Supreme Court, *Edwards v. Aguillard et al.* Where the decision in *McLean* was unappealed, leaving the state of the law unsettled nationally, this subsequent case from Louisiana produced a national rule.

*Edwards* likewise derived from a state public act seeking "balanced Treatment for Creation-Science and Evolution-Science in Public School Instruction". Deviating from the challenged Arkansas statute, however, Louisiana chose not to mandate instruction in either subject. Rather, it insisted that when either is taught, so too must the other be taught. The ground stated for this provision was to defend the pupils' right to be free from indoctrination. While the lower courts treated this case on the model of the *McLean* court's decision and focused largely on the scope of the state's authority to direct the curricula of public schools, the Supreme Court dwelt exclusively on the "religious purpose" test in order to arrive at its overturning decision. In that sense, the court's opinion did not delve into definitions of science.

In fact, though, an argument about the meaning of science lay barely beneath the surface of the opinion. The discredited "religious purpose" constituted in fact only a non-scientific basis for a policy purporting to direct scientific education, which result appeared from the court's heavy reliance upon *McLean*. "The Court found that there can be no legitimate state interest in protecting particular religions from scientific views 'distasteful to them.'"[9] In short, the court's idea of religious purpose was wholly informed by its tacit judgement of what constitutes science, which is wholly compatible with the *McLean* definition:

> We do not imply that a legislature could never require that scientific critiques of prevailing scientific theories be taught ... teaching a variety of scientific theories about the origins of humankind to schoolchildren might be validly done with the clear secular intent of enhancing the effectiveness of science instruction.[10]

The national rule that obtains in the United States, therefore, may be formulated as follows: the public or political determination of the methods, practices and premises of science can be limited by a juridical definition of science, at least insofar as any particular science's methods, practices or premises implicate fundamental guarantees under the Constitution of the United States. Given that present rule, it is important to inquire just how far science enjoys autonomy and to what end.

Let us note again, therefore, that in the unappealed *McLean* case the lower court made it very clear that it could defend science only if it *defined* science. Moreover, at the similar lower court level in the *Aguillard* case the same result was averted only by a ruse: the Appeals Court decided that state authorities *could* define science and remanded the case for such a determination.[11] While that district court opinion avoided the need to define science, it was reversed on appeal, preparing the way for a State Supreme Court to affirm the authority of the Board of Elementary and Secondary Education.[12] The appeal of that decision (recognizing legislative authority) eventually ripened into the case decided by the U.S. Supreme Court. This dynamic made it unnecessary for the Supreme Court directly to review the case on that level. However, it was patent that either court could review, and correct, a state definition of science.

Thus, we learn that the important question is not whether the theory of evolution is science and the theory of creationism is not science. That is *a* question but not the pertinent question. The great question is, who must decide what science is. The answer is: the court must do so. It may, it will, invoke scientific expertise to answer that question. But the court will decide, not the expert.

Now, that brings us back to Louise Robbins. Her science was eventually exposed as the merest charlatanry. In its pursuit, she even defeated the presentations of experts from the Federal Bureau of Investigation, whose results emerged from some of the best-funded and most disciplined laboratories.

Nevertheless, in 1993's *Daubert v. Merrell Dow*, the Supreme Court vindicated Robbins, not her judgements (which remain embarrassing) but her role in the process. For the court defended the judge's authority to determine who was an expert or a scientist independently of third-party criteria ("What is falsifiability?" one asked). Moreover, it may be said that even the facts vindicated Robbins, for we learned following *Daubert* of the scandalous investigative abuses that penetrated the Federal Bureau of Investigation (not to mention many a coroner's and prosecutor's office since), that is, we learned there and elsewhere that consensus procedures assure neither reliability nor ethics. As a result, the only claim science has is no match for a court that promises justice.

## NOTES

1. *Frye v. United States*, 293 F. 1013 (D. C. Cir. 1923).
2. *Daubert v. Merrell Dow*, 509 U.S. 579.
3. *ABA Journal*, August 1995, 81 A.B.A.J.38.
4. *Edwards v. Aguillard*, 482 U.S. 578.
5. *Scopes v. State of Tennessee*, 154 Tenn. 105, 289 S.W. 363 (1927).
6. *McLean v. Arkansas Board of Education*, 529 F. Supp. 1255; 1982 U.S. Dist. LEXIS 10361.
7. Ibid. IV(C).
8. Ibid. IV(D). Emphasis added.
9. Ibid. III(B).
10. Ibid.
11. *Edwards v. Aguillard*, 482 U.S. 578.

12. *Aguillard v. Treen,* 440 So. 2d 704 (La. 1983); *Aguillard v. Treen*, 720 F. 2d. 676 (5th Cir. 1983); *Aguillard v. Edwards*, 765 F. 2d 1251; and *Aguillard v. Edwards*, 778 F. 2d 225.

## REFERENCES

Gibeaut, J. (1999), "Evaluation of a Controversy", *American Bar Association Journal* 85 (November):50.

Hansen, M. (1993), "Believe It or Not", *American Bar Association Journal* 79 (June):64.

*Legal Backgrounder* (1996), Washington Legal Foundation, September 6.

McAree, D. (2002), *National Law Journal* 24(59):A4.

*National Law Journal* (1999), February 8, p. A23.

CHAPTER 4

# The Role of "Expert" Testimony in Court Cases

R.H. McKercher

## INTRODUCTION

When reflecting on my own experience in the court room tendering expert testimony in support of a client's case, I realized that our legal system is far from perfect. The rules are uncertain and the process of selecting the appropriate "expert" leaves much to be desired. Once an expert's testimony is accepted, all too often the evidence is not entirely understood. Indeed, a suspicion remains that the so-called expert testimony was not really the best evidence that might have been advanced.

Reform seems to be on the way, although the speed of reform is hardly breathtaking.

Legal controversies today, whether between individuals or individuals and corporate enterprises or governments, frequently result in court pronouncements that have a significant and far-reaching effect on society as a whole. And often the key evidentiary issue before the court is expert evidence. In recent years expert testimony has exploded in litigation, of whatever kind. Lawsuits depend on expert testimony in criminal cases when DNA (deoxyribonucleic acid) identifies the culprit, cases between farmers and chemical companies, doctors and patients, environmental issues, tax cases, nuclear power generators/ governments and the like.

## WHAT IS "EXPERT" EVIDENCE IN A CIVIL ACTION?

In *R. v. Mohan* (1994),[1] the Supreme Court of Canada heard the appeal of an accused physician who was charged with assaulting four of his female patients. The defence attorney called a psychiatrist to testify whose proffered testimony was designed to prove that the perpetrator of the alleged offence was one of a limited group of individuals who "manifested distinctive abnormal characteristics not possessed by the accused". This testimony was not allowed. On appeal the Supreme Court stated that the test for admissibility of expert testimony was that it must be: (i) relevant, (ii) necessary to assist the trier of facts, (iii) not precluded by an exclusionary rule, and (iv) that of a properly qualified expert.

It is the exclusive prerogative of a trial judge to arrive at findings of fact; therefore, it is critical in the trial process that expert evidence not be misused in such a way as to distort this fact-finding process.

The American Federal Court rules were clarified in 1993 by the U.S. Supreme Court in *Daubert v. Merrell-Dow Pharmaceuticals Inc.*[2] The effect of this decision was described by one commentator as:

> The 1993 decision of the United States Supreme Court in *Daubert v. Merrill Dow Pharm., Inc.* was viewed as a watershed event.... *Daubert* introduced a more elaborate, open-ended approach keyed to validating the reliability and relevance of the methods employed by the expert. The new standard placed increased responsibility on the trial judge who was assigned a gatekeeper's role (Walsh, 1999, p. 140).

## A CIVIL ACTION

Whether an "expert" is called to testify or is allowed to testify is dependent upon court rules and the exercise of judicial discretion by the trial judge. A judge is not a truth commissar but a fact-finder and one who applies the law of the day to the facts before the court based on the evidence. Experts are part of that process of fact-finding. Critics of this process contend that experts are biased in favour of their client's case and that "he who pays the piper calls the tune". In the *American Bar Association Journal*, "experts" are advertised in fields as diverse as "Accidents" to "Utilities". Indeed, some experts spend their time fully occupied as professional witnesses in court proceedings.

While most jurisdictions allow a trial judge to appoint a court-designated expert, or an assessor to advise the judge, such appointments are infrequent. Under such circumstances, can it be said that the current legal system offers the proper evidentiary base of expert testimony to allow the court to arrive at a just result between contending parties? What about important decisions affecting society as a whole?

In a 1987 critique of the American system, Pamela Louise Johnston observed that shopping for a scientific expert is relatively easy and that a lawyer will only call an expert whose views agree with his party's position and discards experts with views that do not agree. This is deemed a "manipulation" by the commentator, which is followed by the observation:

> Thus, if the truth-seeking process is not accurate, the legal system risks hindering or misdirecting economic and technological development. Just as disregarding scientific evidence completely can have these dangers, so can the current practice of expert shopping, which results in each side presenting one-sided expert testimony in court. This practice introduces inaccuracy into the truth-seeking process, corrupting the legal system (Johnston, 1987, para 251).

Recommendations for reform suggested the use of court-appointed experts.

## USE OF EXPERT TESTIMONY

Following *Mohan*, trial judges in Canada have rejected more frequently than before proposed expert testimony. The purpose of this paper is not to become immersed in court rules governing the use of expert testimony. The adversarial system causes one side, if not both, to call expert witnesses reflecting all too often conflicting views on scientific matters. Regrettably, trial judges are often left in a state of bewilderment.

> Much can be said concerning the use of experts who assist the trial judge. The court owes a duty to be scientifically correct as well as legally correct, and the judge in an adversary system is apt to encounter each side presenting skilled experts who present quite persuasively opposite views. He may find himself somewhat bewildered. However, if he has beside him on the bench experts whom the parties agree are impartial, he will have the benefit of their guidance in the understanding of the evidence, and no less important, the restraint of their presence will serve to dampen the enthusiasm of the adversary expert witness (Haines, 1973, p. 51).

The court system has changed very little since those observations were made. Mr. Justice Ian Binnie of the Supreme Court of Canada delivered a lecture at the University of Toronto on February 26, 2003, entitled *Innovation and the Law*. In the course of his remarks, Justice Binnie categorized scientific evidence issues before the courts as "the incomprehensible chasing the unteachable". The point, of course, is that, when an expert scientist sits in the witness box, he or she is talking to a layman in the field of science. Without a basic understanding of the science in question, a judge who is a generalist has a difficult task in order to grasp the full meaning and significance of the testimony, particularly in a highly technical field. This is also true of a jury in jury trials.

The issues that face the courts in cases involving scientific testimony are:

– The best qualified expert is not always the person who provides the testimony.
– Experts are chosen by party litigants for testimony favourable to each side and not simply to provide scientific evidence to the court.
– Under the current system in North America, experts are not necessarily independent, or as independent as they ought to be.
– Judges and juries often are not fully able to comprehend the scientific issues, let alone the solutions and difficult scientific controversy.

Justice Ian Binnie spoke of the need to improve the underlying scientific understanding of the court relative to the subject at hand. He suggested that a panel of experts should be available to assist the court and pointed to the panel of experts available to advise the National Energy Board of Canada.

Justice Steven Breyer of the U.S. Supreme Court observed that judges are typically generalists and are in need of dependable advice from experts (Breyer, 2000). He noted that the President of the United States works with a science advisor and that Congress solicits advice from the National Academy of Sciences on topics involving policy. In the case of American federal judges, the Federal Judicial Center collaborates with the National Academy of Sciences in developing the Academy's program in science, technology and the law.

In recent years in the United States, there has been a serious effort on the part of both the scientific and legal communities to bridge the gap between them. The American legal journal, *Judicature*, published in 1999 a symposium issue focusing on DNA developments and the courts. A series of articles dealt with genes, the new genetics, the role of the courts in sorting out the multiplicity of issues relating to new discoveries, gene therapy and the complexity of scientific evidence and all that means in relation to both civil and criminal cases.

Zweig and Cowdrey state that "judges need a special form of science education in order to craft and implement adjudication tailored to novel, complex cases" (1999, p. 157).

The Woolf Commission in Great Britain was established by the Lord Chancellor to overhaul rules applicable in British courts in the mid-1990s. The commission concluded in 1996 that the use of experts was a major problem in the civil justice system, that such use contributed to the cost of litigation, the increased complexity of the proceedings, as well as delaying proceedings, all of which were found to be offensive to the commissioner. The report recommended that there be a single expert where possible and that the duty of the expert to the court should be emphasized.

> As a general principle, *single experts* should be used wherever the case (or the issue) is concerned with a substantially established area of knowledge and where it is *not* necessary for the court directly to sample a range of opinions (Woolf, 1996, Rec. 167).

Both Australia and New Zealand have followed the Woolf Commission recommendations concerning the use of expert testimony. Canada lags behind the other countries.

Justice Binnie and Justice Breyer, along with others, have observed that an increasingly efficient case-management technique at pre-trial conferences narrows the scientific issues in dispute and, with the assistance of specially trained law clerks, scientific masters or judicially appointed independent experts, the court may well be put in a much stronger position to understand the issues.

There are several sources of scientific information available to the courts on an organized basis. In the United States, the Private Adjudication Center at Duke University provides a registry of independent scientific and technical experts who are willing to provide advice to courts or service court-appointed experts (Breyer, 2000). Perhaps this concept could be used in Canada, as in the case of Duke University, with a panel of experts so that judges can indeed become informed and then arrive at informed decisions in the growing field of scientific knowledge relevant to judicial issues.

Judges do use the Internet for information and knowledge. This in itself suggests the prospect of judicial confusion or misunderstanding if left unclarified by the litigants or their respective experts. If the parties or their lawyers do not know what information has been received by the judge, it is impossible to reach them and affect the outcome of the case. Somehow there must be a flow of information between scientific experts, judges and the concerned parties so that all can understand the fundamental issue before the court and the basis of the judge's decisions.

## CONCLUSIONS

The Canadian and American court systems currently rely on experts who are hired to represent their clients. A better system would allow judges to participate in the process of determining who the best qualified expert is under all the circumstances of the case. A panel of recognized experts would make that task significantly less difficult, assuming such a panel of experts can be developed in any given area of scientific knowledge and that a fair process can be arrived at whereby an expert is selected from such a list. It is hoped that this will allow more authoritative decision-making in the courts, particularly where the outcome of the case decides not only the rights of the parties to the case, but society as a whole.

By developing better training for judges and requiring *independent* expert evidence, Canadian courts will be better able to understand the "ways of science and the ethical, as well as practical and legal aspects of scientific testimony" (Breyer, 2000, p. 6).

## NOTES

1. *R. v. Mohan* (1994) 2. S.C.R. 9.
2. *Daubert v. Merrell-Dow Pharmaceuticals, Inc.*, No. 92-102 (U.S. 06/28/1993), Argued March 30, 1993; Decided June 28, 1993.

## REFERENCES

Breyer, S. (2000), "Science in the Courtroom", *Issues in Science and Technology Online* (summer). 7 pages.

Haines, E.L. (1973), "The Medical Profession and the Adversary Process", *Osgoode Hall Law Journal* 11(1):41-53.

Johnston, P.L. (1987), "Court-Appointed Scientific Expert Witnesses: Unfettering Expertise", *High Technology Law Journal* 2(2).

Walsh, J.T. (1999), "Keeping the Gate: The Evolving Role of the Judiciary in Admitting Scientific Evidence", *Judicature* 83(3):140-143.

Woolf, Lord (1996), *Access to Justice*. Final Report of the Woolf Commission. London: HMSO, July 26.

Zweig, F. and Cowdrey, D.E. (1999), "Educating Judges for Adjudication of New Life Technologies", *Judicature* 83(3):157-161.

CHAPTER 5

# Human Error, Medicine and the Courts

A.F. Merry

In March 2003, a "Perspective" by Edward W. Campion in the *New England Journal of Medicine* began as follows: "Last month, a 17-year-old girl died at Duke University Medical Center after receiving a heart-lung transplant from an incompatible donor. Her blood type was O, the donor's was A, and the mismatch was not recognized until after the transplant operation was over. In rare situations, ABO-incompatible transplantations have been performed intentionally. But in this case it was not intentional. A severe rejection reaction and multiple complications followed, and the patient died" (Campion, 2003).

This story had a particularly poignant background. The girl's father was a truck driver from Mexico and her family, with the assistance of a North Carolina businessman, had exhibited extraordinary resourcefulness and persistence in raising the money from the public to pay for her surgery.

The mistake received wide publicity. Dr. Duane Davis, surgical director of the transplantation program, was quoted as saying "The worst aspect was that the patient became secondary to the conflict between caregivers and the patient's supporters. As the patient died, there were wild accusations charged with animosity." This is not surprising. At the heart of any case involving the death of a young person lies immense personal suffering. It is unrealistic to expect a dispassionate response from a parent who has lost a child to a mistake. Campion encapsulated the probable aftermath of the situation by saying "In our medical world, errors plus animosity usually result in lawsuits" (Campion, 2003).

There are many whose first response to this proposition would be that it was entirely reasonable. A mistake has been made and a patient has died; clearly therefore, someone must be to blame. Furthermore, the courts are the appropriate place in which to hold that person accountable.

Retribution is a valid objective of any legal system, and the notion of an eye for an eye is deeply embedded in most cultures. However, sophisticated modern jurisdictions tend to temper this objective with the principle that justice is important, and often put greater emphasis on the deterrent value of punishment than on retribution for its own sake. Therefore, before accepting the proposition that aggressive litigation is necessarily appropriate when a patient has been inadvertently harmed in the course of medical treatment, it is necessary to consider two important matters which may cast a different light on the issue.

First, there is a matter of public policy. The cost of litigation is in fact part of the overhead of health care. In the end it will be borne by those who must pay for medical care, which (directly or indirectly) means the patients. It is ironic that most societies emphasize prudence in the management of resources for the provision of health care, but appear to throw caution to the winds when it comes to the legal response to iatrogenic harm. An action in the courts can be very expensive, and may not represent good value for money that might be better spent on improving the quality of health care and reducing the likelihood of adverse events recurring in the future.

Secondly, there is a matter of science. There is a strong argument that an unsophisticated rush to find a scapegoat in such circumstances is in fact unscientific. Identifying and eliminating the individual "who is to blame" would be rational if the scientific evidence suggested that iatrogenic harm was exceptional and attributable to the incompetence or carelessness of a few isolated practitioners. However, the evidence is overwhelmingly to the contrary. A number of studies have examined the extent and nature of iatrogenic harm. Of these, the Harvard Medical Practice Study is the best known (Brennan, Leape *et al.*, 1991). It involved structured reviews of 30,121 randomly selected case records from 51 randomly selected acute care non-psychiatric hospitals in the state of New York in 1984. Adverse events were identified in 3.7 per cent of admissions. A report from the influential Institute of Medicine summarized the findings of this and other studies by suggesting that between 44,000 and 98,000 people die annually in the United States as a result of medical errors. The data are somewhat imprecise, but the overall message is clear: iatrogenic harm is not the province of a few "bad apples"; at a national level it occurs alarmingly often. The obvious inference is that it is highly probable that a harmful error in patient management will eventually occur during the course of the career even of a careful and competent practitioner (given his or her treatment of many thousands of patients).

This is particularly distressing because very few doctors go to work with the intention of harming patients. The exceptions, such as Harold Shipman, the English general practitioner who murdered 215 of his patients (Dyer, 2002), are very rare. In fact, most doctors aim for something more than *primum non nocere*: their *raison d'être* is to contribute positively to their patients' well-being, to cure them of their diseases and to enhance their health. This is in contrast to many non-medical accidents in which the intention of the person causing the accident is simply neutral. For example, the motorist who inadvertently runs over a pedestrian may not have intended any harm, but neither did he or she begin with the aim of actually helping the injured person. The Duke case illustrates this point perfectly; the investment in attempting to cure the patient was immense and the outcome went beyond the incidental tragedy of a road traffic accident and amounted to an abject failure of medical care. Over and above the tragic loss of human life, this event involved a monumental loss of credibility for the surgeon, the institution and the team; even if one assumed complete heartlessness on their parts, it is obvious that self-interest alone would have ensured that all concerned would have been at pains to avoid an accident of this type. It is not in their professional self-interest for doctors to harm their patients.

The situation with lawyers is, interestingly, a little different. This is because the legal system (at least in Commonwealth countries and the United States) is adversarial. Most legal and quasi-legal processes involve prosecution and defence. It follows that lawyers working in the courts are often engaged in pursuing a result that is expressly against the interests of at least one of the parties represented in any case. Whereas the need to co-operate with colleagues in the interests of a patient is deeply ingrained in the medical psyche, it seldom seems that lawyers on opposite sides of a dispute have much commitment to the pursuit of each other's clients' interests. The pursuit of "win-win" solutions does not appear to be the norm. On the contrary, the emotional and financial costs are often very high for both parties, and the result is "lose-lose".

Notwithstanding this impression, it is my experience that many lawyers, especially amongst the judiciary, are committed to obtaining just and sensible outcomes from the law, and are disturbed by its limitations, and in particular by some of the consequences of its adversarial nature. They may feel that the law is the best system available, but they recognize that it often fails to serve the interests of those who turn to it when in trouble. Much the same could be said of doctors, many of whom are very much aware of the shortcomings of health care today, and distressed by the sometimes overwhelming impediments to the provision of safe, appropriate and effective health service to those who actually need it. It seems therefore, that patients, doctors and lawyers working in the medical field actually share a common goal: safe outcomes from health care. What is it, then, that hinders us from working together toward our mutual objective?

It is important to begin with a reminder that this goal is actually achieved most of the time. It is not the case that either system fails everyone, rather that the failures that do occur are often very painful and very visible.

Having said this, there are a number of impediments to just and effective outcomes from the legal response to iatrogenic harm. One of these impediments relates to a gap in perception. The law amounts to a man-made set of rules based upon a theoretical view of the world as it ought to be. There is therefore a tendency for lawyers to see the world in this way. Science, including medical science, attempts to deal with the world as it is. Doctors are accustomed to the realities of medical practice, and therefore tend to be somewhat mystified by lay expectations of perfection.

This does not mean that lawyers always fail to recognize the importance of a sophisticated understanding of the world as it is, anymore than it implies a complete lack of insight into the legal issues on the part of doctors. The difficulties often arise not so much from the theoretical underpinnings of the law, but rather from the practical implementation of these principles in the real world of the courts. For this, both lawyers and doctors must take responsibility. It is clear that judges and juries cannot themselves be experts in every branch of science, and must therefore depend primarily on expert witnesses. It follows that there is a heavy responsibility on expert witnesses (in the case of medical lawsuits, these will usually be doctors) to provide disinterested and comprehensive advice about the world as it actually is. What is perhaps less obvious is that there is also a responsibility on the part of the lawyers to facilitate the efforts of the experts in providing this advice within the very formal, often unfamiliar, often threatening and often disempowering environment of the courts. Regrettably, the rules of evidence and the adversarial nature of civil, criminal or disciplinary proceedings often tend to hinder rather than help the process of illumination.

Further impediments to the legal process are to be found in the many barriers to successful expert testimony. One of these barriers in particular is relevant to the topic, Science in the Courts. In general, the evidence admissible in a court is factual. The evidence of those involved with any particular event is restricted to what they saw or experienced. Opinion is not admissible. The exception to this rule is the opinion of an expert. However, in order for expert testimony to be admissible, it is a requirement that this evidence concerns something that is not simply a matter of everyday experience. If a judge and jury can be expected to understand the matter on the basis of their own, non-expert, experience of the world, then expert evidence is not admissible. On the face of it, human error seems to be just that, a matter of everyday experience. It is very tempting to assume that we all understand human error, on the grounds that we have all experienced it. On the contrary, however, there is actually a substantial body of theoretical, empirical and experimental scientific knowledge about human error, its causation and its avoidance, and the facts are highly technical and often counter-intuitive. Expert evidence is called for in evaluating medical errors and this point is not always understood by the courts.

A story published in a New Zealand newspaper some years ago is illustrative (Merry and McCall Smith, 2001, pp 77-78). This story involved an expert and a novice. The expert was a hang-gliding instructor under whose tutelage the novice was to experience a tandem flight (given to him by his fiancée as a present). While securing the harness the expert (i.e., the instructor) was distracted by a puff of wind and failed to fasten it correctly. The result was that, on launching, the instructor fell some ten metres or so, injuring himself and leaving his novice passenger to soar out on his own into the sky, no doubt contemplating the fact that this was a present from his fiancée. The novice crashed into the sea below, narrowly missing a fisherman. Injuries were sustained by the instructor and his passenger, but they were not life threatening.

This story permits a number of points to be made. First, experts make errors. This, I think, is not intuitive. Indeed, it often seems that expertise is thought somehow to justify an expectation of error-free performance. The reality is that expertise does reduce the risk of error, but it does not eliminate it. Training, skill and knowledge reduce the total number of errors and also alter the type of errors a person is likely to make. Surprisingly, experts are actually more likely to make certain types of error then novices, although they make fewer errors overall. Specifically, they are more likely to make errors of the type known as skill-based (slips or lapses), and less likely to make errors of the types known as rule-based. Most skilled human tasks depend on semi-automatic learned responses to particular situations, a combination of skill-based and rule-based activities. The response of an expert rugby player who has been passed the ball will require skill, but it will also require several almost instantaneous decisions. These will depend on his reducing the particular (unique) situation to a more generic representation, or schema, and matching this with schemata previously stored in his memory on the basis of training and past experience, and all with very little conscious effort. Given situation X, the player knows on the basis of a rule that the correct response is Y. Driving a motor car is similar; decisions in traffic are seldom made by thinking matters through from first principles, there simply is not time. That is why novices find traffic very challenging. Similar considerations apply to medical endeavours such as surgery or anaesthesia. To be successful, it is necessary that situations are recognized as being roughly equivalent to ones previously encountered so that responses can be made almost instantly, on the basis of experience. Novices lack the store of rules to permit these semi-automatic responses, and the development of expertise is largely about building up a store of such rules, and learning to apply them semi-automatically. Expertise implies the synthesis of individual actions into complex tasks, which are carried out as integrated units of activity. Tying one's shoe laces is like this. If one is distracted halfway through this task, many people find it necessary to start again at the beginning: the activity is stored within memory as a complete unit, not as a set of separate steps. Getting dressed involves a relatively small number of complex tasks like this, rather than a large number of individual actions. The whole process can be completed with little if any thought, while simultaneously planning the day, listening to the radio and drinking a cup of coffee. However, if distracted, there is a risk of losing one's place in the sequence, and omitting a key step, particularly if that step was in some way exceptional. For example, if distracted at the critical moment, known as a *decision node*, one might forget an important detail, such as the need to put one's wallet into a jacket pocket before leaving the house. This is known as a lapse. The hang-gliding instructor's error was a lapse. Similarly, giving the wrong drug (a common problem in most studies of iatrogenic harm) is often the result of a lapse. It is likely that the events at Duke involved a lapse.

The second point illustrated by this story is that errors of this type are not necessarily evidence of carelessness. It is a reasonable assumption that the hang-gliding instructor cared about the prospect of falling from the hang-glider. The corollary is that deterrence is useless in preventing errors of this type. If the potential of plummeting to your death from a hang-glider will not deter you from an error of this type, draconian law is unlikely to be effective. The influence of outcome on our judgement of accountability can also be seen in this example. Had someone died in this accident it is likely, in New Zealand at that time, that manslaughter charges would have been laid. As it was, the incident simply became the subject of an amusing newspaper article, although the instructor was prosecuted on a more minor charge.

An error may be defined as "the unintentional use of a wrong plan to achieve an aim, or the unintentional failure to carry out a planned action as intended" (Runciman, Merry and Tito, 2003). In simple language, this may be thought of as trying to do the right thing but actually doing the wrong thing. The focus in this definition is on the process involved, not on the outcome. The key word is *unintentional*. This distinguishes an error from a violation, which involves choice; that is, it is intentional. A violation may be defined as "a deliberate — but not necessarily reprehensible — deviation from those practices appreciated by the individual as being required by regulation, or necessary or advisable to achieve an appropriate objective while maintaining safety and the ongoing operation of a device or system" (Merry and McCall Smith, 2001, p 101). Again, the definition focuses on the mental state and actions involved, not on the outcome.

The distinction between an error and a violation can be illustrated by a second story (Williams, 1995). A Canadian anaesthetist left a patient unattended in the operating room while he spoke on the telephone. An airway disconnection occurred and a 17 year-old patient died. The anaesthetist falsified the records. He eventually pleaded guilty and was sentenced to six months in jail. This is not an example of error; it is an example of violation. Violations may reflect carelessness and deterrence may be effective in preventing them. However, not all violations are reprehensible. Sometimes violations are forced on people by the systems in which they work. Situations of this type are known as double-binds. For example, it may be thought a violation to work when excessively fatigued, but there are many occasions in which health practitioners find it difficult to avoid this.

The legal concept of negligence is usually expressed in terms of a failure to use reasonable knowledge, skill and care. The question arises of how this relates to errors and violations, and of the test used for negligence. The usual legal test is one of reasonableness. However, this may be misleading. The writer A.P. Herbert described the reasonable man as "an odious individual". The problem is that error is never reasonable in hindsight; the difficulty arises from what is tested, the error or the person. A reasonable person may make an error, but the error is not likely to be thought reasonable. To make matters worse, experts tend to describe the standard of care which *ought to be* observed rather than the standard that *is* commonly observed (again we see a difference between the world as it is and the world as people would like it to be). How then can one know more about the standard that actually is observed? From science. For example, one might not think it reasonable for an anaesthetist to administer the wrong drug to a patient. A survey conducted in New Zealand indicated that 89 per cent of anaesthetists had given the wrong drug at some stage during their careers. If these data are accepted, it follows either that giving the wrong drug must be something which a reasonable anaesthetist can do or that only 11 per cent of anaesthetists are reasonable.

In his judgement in *Whitehouse v. Jordan*, an obstetrics negligence case, Lord Denning observed that an error of judgement in a professional context did not amount to negligence. To test this, he said, "one might ask the average competent and careful practitioner: 'Is this sort of mistake that you might have made?' If he says: 'Yes, even doing the best I could, it might have happened to me', then it is not negligent" (Merry and McCall Smith, 2001, p 172). However, it seems that the judge had made a mistake. At the House of Lords this message was "corrected"; Lord Fraser courteously suggested that what Lord Denning had *meant* to say was that an error of judgement was not *necessarily* negligent. "The true position," Lord Fraser said, "is that an error of judgement may, or may not, be negligent; it depends on the nature of the error." That I think is correct. It is interesting that the law recognizes that errors made during the actual cut and thrust of the case are not necessarily culpable, in effect, that all human beings make mistakes, especially under pressure. Here, at least, the law reflects the real world, perhaps because this world is one inhabited by lawyers.

This brings us back to the story of the death at Duke University. In his commentary, Campion made a telling observation; he said, "In the aftermath of such a disaster there must be an assignment of blame." This may be true, but at least let that assignment of blame be based on a careful appraisal of the facts in the context of our scientific under-standing of the nature of human error, rather than on an unsophisticated belief that the tragic outcome justifies retribution *per se*. This will not be easy and will require much of the legal system and of the scientists the legal system depends upon for advice. The death of this young girl after a surgery intended to save her life, undertaken at one of the most prestigious medical institutions in the world, is a clear illustration of a point made by Atul Gawande about iatrogenic harm in general: "The real problem isn't how to stop bad doctors from harming, even killing, their patients. It's how to prevent good doctors from doing so" (Gawande, 1999).

## REFERENCES

Brennan, T.A., Leape, L.L. *et al.* (1991), "Incidence of Adverse Events and Negligence in Hospitalized Patients — Results of the Harvard Medical Practice Study I", *New England Journal of Medicine* 324(6):370-376.

Campion, E.W. (2003), "A Death at Duke", *New England Journal of Medicine* 348(12):1083-1084.

Dyer, C. (2002), "Shipman Inquiry Calls for Major Changes in Death Certi-fication", *British Medical Journal* 325(7370):919.

Gawande, A. (1999), "When Doctors Make Mistakes", *The New Yorker*, pp. 40-55.

Merry, A. F. and McCall Smith, A. (2001), *Errors, Medicine and the Law*. Cambridge: Cambridge University Press.

Runciman, W.B., Merry, A.F. and Tito, F. (2003), "Error, Blame, and the Law in Health Care: An Antipodean Perspective", *Annals of Internal Medicine* 138(12):974-979.

Williams, L.S. (1995), "Anesthetist Receives Jail Sentence After Patient Left in Vegetative State", *Canadian Medical Association Journal* 153:619-620.

# PART III

## GOVERNMENT AND SCIENCE

CHAPTER 6

# The Roles of Statistics in Government

## J.C. Bailar III

Many issues plague the relationship between science, including statistical science, and government. These include failures on each side to understand the essence of the other, confusion between science (which is rooted in the search for truth) and technology (which assumes that truth is at hand and ready for use) and confusion between information and advice. I will focus here on two topics: the nature and definition of statistics and the giving and receiving of advice. At the end, they will converge on a third theme, academic training. A recurring theme is that science is uncertain: sometimes we just do not know, or even cannot know. Another point that must get less attention than it needs is that the scientific record as a whole can be highly biased even if each piece of the record is well done and unbiased. Uncertainty reigns.

There are many definitions of statistics, but I will explicitly reject two that are valid but seem to have little place in discussions here. I am not concerned with statistics as the compilation of data and their descriptive presentation (as in win-loss records in sports, foreign trade and school completion rates). These have important uses, but in their simplest form, they do not raise serious issues about government and science, including statistics. A second view, often favoured in academic circles, takes statistics as a highly formalized area of study akin to, or even a branch of, mathematics. That view has been highly productive of new ideas and procedures, but as a separate topic it also has little place in discussions of government and science.

I prefer a third view, that statistics is best defined as the art and science of interpreting quantitative data. The key idea is not to collect and present data, nor the reduction of data to simple measures like means, but rather to interpret the data. Art is critical in this because productive interpretation generally requires a context broader than the recorded data, including such matters as when, why and especially how the data were gathered, what things may have gone wrong in the gathering (and things always go wrong to some degree), what is already known about the subject, how new analyses or new data may fit in, how results may be interpreted or misinterpreted (by error or otherwise), what the various users of the analysis think they need, how they will use the statistical information, even whether the results will be accepted as valid. These matters cannot be reduced to rules because they vary widely from problem to problem and because their understanding relies heavily on that uncommon quality called common sense. Most statistical analysis of this kind is, and should be, carried out by persons with little formal training in statistics. In science, and in everyday life, we should be our own statisticians. Education, supervised training and practice can sharpen skills, and I am a strong supporter of increasing the statistical component of the educational system in schools and colleges, beginning with Grade 1. However, there is good reason to develop a group of professional statisticians of adequate size and orientation that will help with bigger and more complex problems, such as a national population census, a complex telephone survey, or a comparison of two medical treatments. Statistical graphics has come to the fore in recent years and here, too, there is need for special training and assistance in finding the right tools and using them to reveal otherwise hidden truths.

Matters that rise to the highest levels of government are weighted with the most difficult issues; simpler things are generally resolved at lower levels unless they involve great expense or great risk. Thus, there is a need, at these high levels, for special competence in statistics as used in interpretation. Some persons are very good at this, and it has been my privilege to work with several of them — Frederick Mosteller, Jerome Cornfield, Chester Bliss and John Tukey, among others. Not all were trained as statisticians (Cornfield was trained in history, Bliss was an entomologist), but all had to educate themselves in how to serve critical national and global needs. They did not learn these things in the classroom nor at the feet of mentors. Self-education, often in the face of pressures to do as one's colleagues do, is a remarkably inefficient way to produce new talent to serve at the highest levels.

This brings me near the end of my first theme: the nature and definition of statistics. The statistical profession should be focused on the art and science of interpreting quantitative data, and our teaching and training programmes should be so oriented. I am particularly concerned about academic departments that provide professional rewards only for theoretical advances, do not try to recruit students with interests beyond the formalized study of mathematical statistics, do not require that students acquire extensive experience with a range of real problems that will develop critical skills and habits of thinking, and do not inculcate attitudes supportive of working on a national or global level. We need some big changes.

This brings me to my second theme: the giving and receiving of advice. Strictly speaking, scientists are asked for advice less often than they are asked to summarize and interpret what is known about some matter, but I will speak about all of this as "advice". When we ask a spouse or friend whether we should return some newly purchased piece of clothing, we may not want nor expect an honest and thoughtful answer. I have seen much scientific advice provided in the same spirit, but the corridor consultation may lead to grave misunderstandings on both sides about the issue as well as the advice offered. Scientific advice regarding major public issues needs much more and can impose significant burdens on both the provider and the recipient. Providers must be well-informed about many aspects of a complex problem, they must make a diligent search for relevant information, they must be as critical and as objective as possible, they must give careful attention and critique to alternative views, especially views that may be unreasonably attractive to the recipients, and they must be brief as well as honest and highly articulate in reporting their findings and conclusions

Recipients, especially when they have requested the advice, also have obligations. A requester must expect to pay the costs of preparing the advice, and must offer political cover if it is needed. The request must be genuine, in that the response will be given careful consideration. The requestor must not use the request solely to delay or divert a difficult or unpleasant decision, must listen carefully, especially when the advice is unexpected or unwelcome, must be sure that it is understood, and must explain any contrary reasoning, especially if the advice is not followed. Honest explanation is always in order when advice is not taken. Advice will generally be received and interpreted in a context that includes many other inputs and constraints: legal, economic and institutional, among others. These may include limits on money, expertise and time available, but perhaps the most pervasive and powerful of influences on the receipt of scientific advice is political. In the halls of the legislatures, the word "political" is not pejorative, and one might agree that in a democratic society, political influences should be well informed and sympathetic to other injustices, but in the end should generally dominate other inputs to the decision processes.

There are exceptions, of course, when a leader bears the costs and risks of acting against the public will of the moment when a greater good beckons, but the combination of real need and real leadership is not common.

What does this all have to do with giving scientific advice? We must remember that our view of the world is not the only one, as important as we may think it is, and that advice may often not be followed for reasons that are valid in a political context. In short, we must expect to lose some fights, sometimes big ones that could be won only by sweeping changes in our systems of democratic governance. Such wins would not be worth the cost.

Even well-developed scientific advice will often be less than clear-cut and is sometimes less than unanimous. It is the job of the science advisor to say, when necessary, "We don't know", or even, "We can never know". The recipient must accept such a response when it comes. One of the great differences between science and politics is that science is concerned primarily with conclusions (regardless of consequences), while politics is concerned primarily with decisions (despite uncertainties). Of course, a decision not to act (or not to act now) is itself a decision of a different sort, even when it is not explicit.

What can scientists and statisticians do to improve government and governmental decisions? This is my third theme: academic training. Schoolchildren are the place to start. Children can and should be taught many things now omitted or dealt with too lightly. Some of the statistical concepts to be introduced early include:

– the pervasive role of randomness in nearly everything that matters;
– the balancing of costs, risks, and benefits, including those not fully identified or understood;
– the evaluation of data for bias, and how to use imperfect data when necessary; and
– the knowledge that random events, including clusters, occur with just the expected frequency, and that the outcomes of independent events are in fact independent.

Many other topics accessible to children, and valuable in everyday life, could be added. One need only look at the pervasive effects of compulsive gambling, the horoscopes in our daily papers, or the television coverage of random but presumably "newsworthy" events to see that there is a problem.

The need for change in statistical education begins in our school days, but continues to more advanced levels, including graduate and postgraduate training, and even the professional atmosphere in which many of us work. In that atmosphere, academics do not spend much of their careers on real problems; bias is not treated as a proper subject for study; professional rewards are based on publications in statistical journals, the more abstract the better; programmes seek students who are interested, and will be good at, continuing the kinds of things their mentors do; little professional credit is given for help in solving "real" national or global problems, regardless of their importance; and we do not provide, and reward, the right kinds of role models.

It appears that these problems go well beyond statistics, and infect the whole range of what we call the hard sciences. Unless, and until, training programmes are changed, science, including statistics, will continue to be outside the main centres of governmental power, called on with less than the optimum frequency, often misunderstood or misinterpreted, and will fall short of what would be ideal in a world that runs more and more on science.

And finally, a few words about the U.S. Office of Technology Assessment (OTA). It was originally established some thirty years ago to provide the two houses of the U.S. Congress with timely, well-targeted information needed for the optimum development of science-related legislation. The OTA made most of their work public and was initially under the direction of a former member of Congress. It worked to the great benefit of that public. About ten years ago, OTA was suddenly, and quite surprisingly, abolished. I have tried to determine the reasons for this unexpected end to a successful programme, and the reasons given have varied widely. Some say that OTA simply outlived its usefulness, which is not very enlightening and, I am sure, not true. Some say that its work became sloppy, or too expensive, or too slow, or was not directed at the problems that Congress had presented. My own view is that OTA remained a source of effective, efficient, well-targeted sound analysis to the end, but was undone by political forces that were unhappy about some of the analyses that undercut programmes favoured by some legislators and administrators. In short, a Republican administration came to believe that OTA was saying too many things that the administration did not want to hear and claimed that the advice was biased by political views from the other side of the spectrum.

I conclude that the administration of that day (like the administration of the present) did not want to deal with any analyses that might be politically inconvenient. Whatever the reason, anyone who is contemplating a similar kind of institutional arrangement to provide scientific analysis and technical advice, including statistics, to government should study the rise and fall of the OTA.

CHAPTER 7

# The Public, Doctors and Government: A Changing Relationship

## D.H. Irvine

I want to talk about the changing relationships between patients and doctors, the public and the medical profession, and government both as a policymaker and employer. The change is international, and the characteristics are to some extent determined by the social culture in the various countries such as Canada, the United States and Australasia. But there are certain common underlying principles. In the United Kingdom our particular brand of revolutionary process acquired momentum in a very public way following a small but high-profile series of medical disasters that undermined public trust and confidence in doctors and the National Health Service (NHS) (Irvine, 1999). The failure of paediatric cardiac surgery in the 1980s and early 1990s at the Bristol Royal Infirmary is the best-known example. But there were several others, including the murders committed by a general practitioner, Dr. Harold Shipman.

It seems sad but true that it often takes a disaster to bring about serious change in structures, organizations and relationships, even though the need for change has often been manifest for some time. Thus, it was similar here, where it took a disaster to cause tectonic plates in the medical profession and government to shift. In this period of substantial change there seems to be three constants for patients: good access to care when it is needed; competent, honest health professionals who will treat people empathetically, with respect, kindness and courtesy; and care provided by a clinical team that can be relied on to provide care of optimum quality and safety. How can these fundamentals be achieved in today's world?

## DRIVERS OF CHANGE

What are the main drivers of change? The most important are medical science, information technology and social change. There are others such as economics and demography, but their effects are more focused.

*Medical science.* The principal driver is medical science itself. Science-based medicine is essentially a creature of the twentieth century, especially the last fifty years or so. It has produced huge benefits for society, evident to all. In the future the pace of scientific discovery and technological development will continue inexorably, with all that implies in terms of better outcomes of care reflected in a better quality of life. But the new science carries with it a health warning. As the paediatrician, Sir Cyril Chantler, put it "medicine used to be simple, ineffective and relatively safe; now it is complex, effective, and potentially dangerous" (Chantler, 1999, p. 1181).

*Information technology.* Today it is the information age as much as medical science that has been driving change. Everyone has direct access through the Internet to the database of medicine, a fact that has altered the power relationship between doctor and patient, in favour of the patient, forever. The globalization of medical practice has already begun. It is high-tech, interventionalist specialities such as transplant and cardiac surgery that are leading the way, as definitive outcomes and risks for specified procedures are being established and made publicly available. On the Internet and in our newspapers one can expect more international, publicly accessible information in future on clinical and professional standards, and comparative data about the clinical performance of individual doctors, clinical teams and health-care institutions, and of patients' experiences of them. Consumer and patient groups are contributing to these developments, helping to drive them. The Internet and the media have just as surely transformed patient connections and communications about health care worldwide and therefore their ability to influence their performance and practices of clinicians.

*Social mores.* The third big driver derives from changing public attitudes, expectations and general societal culture. Fifty years ago, when the NHS was started, patients had a deferential attitude to professionals, especially doctors. In the main they were passive, uncritical and submissive, very much the junior partner in the doctor-patient relationships. There was unquestioning trust, "doctor knows best". The profession was trusted to regulate itself with minimum accountability.

A consequence of this "producer-led" relationship was that medicine was essentially how doctors interpreted it.

But this is no longer true. Today we live in a consumer society in which, in terms of service, the patient comes first. More people are better educated, and expect to be in charge of their lives. We see this kind of social change expressed in health care in terms of the "autonomous patient" (Coulter, 2002), in which it is the patient rather than the professional who is in ultimate charge and who makes the ultimate decisions. Now the expectation is that health care will be seen primarily "through the eyes of the patient". There is then a different, more robust approach to quality of service, accountability and transparency of process.

It has been the social drivers, more than the scientific and technological drivers, that have proved to be the most challenging and provocative for doctors.

## THE KEY ELEMENTS

Let me now try to give a flavour of where the cycle of change stands in the United Kingdom, and what might be expected for the immediate future. There are four key elements: acceptance of the fact of the autonomous patient; a reorientation of the medical culture, a new professionalism in medicine; changes to medical regulations; and changes to the structure and organization of the NHS as consumer choice begins to bite. Underlying each of these is the fact that the strong consensual, often collusive, relationship between the medical profession and the state through the NHS in the United Kingdom is being challenged by a hitherto weak third force, the public/consumer patient factor. One implication is that the medical profession is now having to think about how it establishes a much more direct relationship with the public rather than have it mediated through government.

### Patient Autonomy

In the United Kingdom, we have yet to see the effects of the fully empowered autonomous patient. Patient autonomy will find its ultimate expression in the exercise of choice. Yet in the NHS, choice has been relatively limited hitherto. In health care, as in all our public services, equity of entitlement and access has been prized above all; everyone is entitled to the same. It has brought huge benefits, even though in practice distribution and quality have often been far from equitable.

There is today a shift from egalitarianism to personal autonomy in all walks of life. Health care is no exception. In real life, when one is confronted with serious illness in the family, there is a need to do the best for our loved ones. Equity is put to one side in order to try to get the best doctor and the best treatment. Choice is exercised only when possible. The pressure to broaden the scope for choice is bound to increase as more and more people feel that they should have that opportunity, particularly as they gain access to more and better information about the technical performance of individual doctors and the results of clinical care in individual hospital units and general practice. That will be the patient's starting point for making informed decisions about care: who, where, what, which, how. The trend carries with it huge consequences for the quality, provision and the organization of health services, for regulation and for the culture of professionalism to which I shall come in a moment. It has equally profound implications for our responsibilities, as citizens, to those people who have the same individual right to choice, but who for economic and other reasons are least able to exercise it. Because the trend toward more choice is unstoppable there is an urgent need now for serious public debate and examination of the subject and all its ramifications.

## *New Professionalism*

Professionalism should be the mirror image of public expectations. Professional culture should express and reflect professional values and standards, which embody societal expectations and mores that exist at any one time. What has happened in this country in recent years is that the medical culture in some important respects has not kept pace with changing societal values and expectations. In particular, as the United Kingdom has moved from being a producer-dominated to a consumer-led society, the medical profession is slow to recognize the significance of the changing power relationship, and all that implied, between doctors and patients. That particular societal change is well illustrated in the changing public attitudes to consent to treatment. Here, the position has moved from where doctors were granted huge licence by patients to do what they thought was necessary to the position now where consent has become a metaphor for patient autonomy and respect as well as specific permission for some procedure or treatment. The profession, failing to understand the full significance of this societal change, was resentful of it. Inevitably the gap between societal values and expectations and medical values widened to a point where conflict and loss of trust became inevitable.

In this era of changing relationships, I regard professionalism as the key to the future relationship among practitioners, the public and employers (Irvine, 2003). Looking back we have learned, somewhat to our cost, that too often doctors have regarded their professionalism rather narrowly, as a dry ethical concept rather than the contemporary embodiment of their culture. True professionalism embodies not only values and standards with which society is comfortable, but also the determination to see that these are practised in full by all individual doctors and by the profession collectively.

A fundamental breakthrough came in the United Kingdom when the General Medical Council, which regulates the medical profession, abandoned virtually unrestricted clinical autonomy for individual doctors in favour of a clear set of principles, which embraced current societal expectations. These principles, expressed in a code *Good Medical Practice* (General Medical Council, 1999) were established on the basis of a consensus derived from full public involvement. They represent a definitive statement of duties and responsibilities that both the public and the medical profession expect of doctors. To give them teeth, these duties and responsibilities have been linked to a doctor's licence to practise and the maintenance of that licence has been made contingent on continuing compliance through a process of verification called revalidation. Thus, there is now a statement of doctors' duties and responsibilities that go with their rights and privileges. In other words we have, in essence, the professional side of a new regulative bargain between the public and the profession.

How does this new professionalism differ from the old? It starts by recognizing the centrality of the autonomous patient. That is the fundamentally different point of departure. A sound ethical foundation, scientific and technical competence, the interests of the patient and a notion of service are still core values. But the new professionalism embraces evidence-based medicine rather than clinical pragmatism, the recognition of the fundamental importance of attitude and behaviour, of partnership with patients, and physician accountability rather than personal autonomy. At the same time, the new professionalism is about teamwork rather than individualism, collective as well as personal responsibility, transparency rather than secrecy, empathetic communication and above all respect for others. It involves an unreserved commitment to quality improvement through clinical governance. In short, the profession of medicine must become, as Eliot Freidson, the sociologist, has said that enthused with the spirit of openness, driven by the conviction that one's decisions must be routinely opened to inspection and evaluation, like the openness that pervades science and scholarship (Freidson, 1994).

New thinking about professionalism means re-thinking our medical institutions: our medical colleges, the professional societies and the role of our university medical schools. In embedding the new professionalism I have argued that these institutions of medicine now have a unique opportunity, indeed an obligation, to re-think their purpose, functions and organizations in ways that, individually and together, will help them to cement the partnership and secure the new settlement between the profession and the public.

A more confident, more assertive profession, working with and for the public, should play a more influential and proactive role in shaping the future direction of medicine, explaining its limits as well as its potential. The notion of the profession accepting a civic duty of this kind would contribute to the building of public confidence and trust. I believe that if we follow this kind of holistic road to professionalism, the public and the profession together could revolutionize the practice of medicine. This is indeed the thinking not only in the United Kingdom but in Canada, Australasia and the United States.

## The Importance of Independent Regulation

As part of the new settlement we are discovering why professional and health-care regulation in future needs to be robustly independent of any sectoral interest. The combination of rigorous regulation, modern professionalism, expressed through good clinical governance, and the ability of autonomous patients to make well-informed choices about their health care offers the best way of assuring quality in future.

In the United Kingdom, the regulators of the individual health professions, which provide the framework for professionalism in their respective fields, have been recently reconstructed around the principles of modern governance. Their accountability for carrying out their task effectively is to be strengthened. An overarching co-ordinating body has been established. And for the first time in the United Kingdom we have an independent regulator for our health-care institutions, the Commission for Health Improvement, shortly to become the Commission for Health Audit and Inspection.

In the more pluralistic approach to the provisions of health care these steps are welcome. But to my mind they do not go far enough. I believe that we have yet to evolve a mechanism that gives the public direct access, through Parliament, to the regulators taking decisions on their behalf. I would have preferred that Parliament think imaginatively about how this might best be done, what might be an improvement on the existing arrangements through select committees. I have already suggested an all-party committee, drawn from both houses of Parliament, which would be well supported administratively. Whichever method emerges, accountability should flow in future from the information the regulators would be required to make available publicly about their stewardship of their part of the regulatory system. I believe that this openness would be enhanced by the scrutiny of the results in public, and at the same time by independent press scrutiny, and that these would become an inherent part of the process.

## More Diverse Provision

The last ten years has seen various experiments with attempts to free up the provision of health care in our hospitals and general practices from over-strong central control. Despite experiments with NHS Trusts and now Foundation Hospitals, there is a general feeling that the central control mechanisms are still too strong. The NHS still has low expectations of its performance because, being centrally driven and controlled the opportunities for organizational innovation and individual professional initiative and development are limited and inevitably will remain so. Given that we aspire to be an international leader in health care, I do not believe this is a sustainable position either for the patients who use the NHS or for the practice and the morale of the people who work in it.

I believe that we will now have to discard this centralized bureaucratic straight-jacket. We need a more flexible system of health care whose only purpose is to serve people in need and which will meet the expectations of the autonomous patient. In essence, we need ministers of the Crown to leave the business of managing the health-care profession to others, unconnected directly with government, who can give it their undivided attention and commitment. The organization and management of health care should not be a function of politicians. That is not to say that government does not have real responsibilities. Health care will always be political and governments have real responsibilities in, for example, resolving the big strategic issues in health such as how we pay for health care, what we are prepared to afford and how we reconcile individual choice with the need to protect those who are less able to look after themselves. There is a need to look beyond the provision of health care to the much bigger picture of public health itself and how the nation is to become healthier. Politicians should be leading the debate about how these important issues of public policy, ethics and strategy are to be resolved, with Parliament setting the parameters and framework within which providers function. In this scenario, ministers would be unequivocally on the side of patients and the regulators, not the providers. And the health professionals in hospitals and primary care would have much more freedom to deliver the services required of them in ways that provide the best outcomes for patients and for themselves.

## CONCLUSION

Much is changing but more change is still to come. What has not changed is the fact that the public wants and needs doctors who are knowledgeable and skilled, ethical and committed. To this end a new kind of professionalism in medicine is evolving that is firmly grounded in the public interest and in a partnership between the public and the profession itself.

## REFERENCES

Chantler, C. (1999), "The Role and Regulation of Doctors in the Delivery of Healthcare", *Lancet* 353:1178-1181.

Coulter, A. (2002), *The Autonomous Patient: Ending Paternalism in Medical Care*. London: The Nuffield Trust.

Friedson, E. (1994), *Professionalism Reborn: Theory, Prophecy and Policy*. Cambridge: Polity Press.

General Medical Council (1999), *Good Medical Practice*. London: GMC.

Irvine, D. (1999), "The Performance of Doctors: The New Professionalism", *Lancet* 353:1174-1177.

_____ (2003), *The Doctors' Tale: Professionalism and Public Trust*. Oxford: Radcliffe Medical Press.

CHAPTER 8

# Government and Feces, or Feces Isn't What It Used to Be

M.S. McQuigge

It has been three years since the Walkerton water disaster was caused by a newly emerging bacteria called *E.coli O157:H7*. Since then, I have watched, and sometimes been involved in, how the Ontario government has reacted to that event (McQuigge, 2002).

First, the public did not see the government as dealing well with the event, either before, during or after. Walkerton has become a political liability and is best not talked about in government circles.

Secondly, many issues are unresolved. For example: What will be the future source for Walkerton's water? Will individuals who were ill with *E. coli O157:H7* have their future health adversely affected? But mostly, for some of us involved, the concern is the prevention of future disasters of this kind. And it is on this last question that scientific communication and government decision-making has been put to the test.

## NOW WE HAVE FAST SCIENCE AND SLOW LAWS

*E.coli O157:H7* was discovered in 1982 and a great deal is now known about the bacteria. It has mutated from harmless *E.coli,* which thrives in the stomach, to become a cause of disease that can be a killer. Its genetic structure is known, as well as the genes that make it kill. This bacterium is now present in at least 10 per cent of calf manure across Canada and has recently been found in chickens and pigs. There are weekly public health reports of illness caused by this bacterium in our food. And rarely, but significantly, it is found in the drinking water. Scientists have a notion of what can kill it; and a vaccine against it is being tested in cattle. All this has evolved, from a scientific perspective, in a relatively short time.

After the Walkerton disaster, the subsequent inquiry and the recommendations from the commissioner of the inquiry, it was assumed that laws would be designed to prevent a future disaster. Some have. But it will take eight or more years to see protective measures put in place. The Ontario government, which was going to enact a new nutrient (manure) management law has postponed it until at least 2008. We now have fast science and slow law.

Why the delay? This is a politically sensitive issue. Farmers with small farms are very concerned that meeting the costs of new manure regulations will put them out of business. They see the new law as being designed for large, intensive farming businesses and not tailored to small farms. Water regulations are resisted by small water distribution managers because the regulations are perceived as being lumped into regulations designed for large water distribution systems and the costs, if not shared by the government, are prohibitive.

The farming lobby has been working overtime in resisting new manure-management laws. The lobby certainly does not want the name "manure" to be changed to feces or septage, or environmental contaminant and potential killer. The name has the nice connotation of a fertilizer sprinkled on the rose garden. And that is where the scientific voice is almost non-existent. What has not been conveyed to the public and, through them, to the politicians, is that feces is not what it used to be. In fact, *E.coli O157:H7* is just one of many serious pollutants in animal feces. Salmonella, *Cryptosporidium, Listeria*, antibiotic resistant bacteria and many others that can cause serious disease are now regular inhabitants of manure.

For centuries, animal and human manures have been spread on the land and this has become an accepted practice. Now, this practice poses a serious threat to our waterways and groundwater in that it can contaminate the drinking water. And I do not think the public understands that yet. This is normal. In management practice, it takes about eight years for change to be accepted and percolate through an organization. But here, lives, not a business culture, are at stake. Failure to protect our water and food will lead to lives lost. If politics is the art of the possible, this will happen because governments will try to balance their chances of being re-elected with the need to protect the public's health and safety.

# WHERE IS THE SCIENTIFIC VOICE?

Is the role of scientists to do the science and then sit back and see what happens or is it their moral duty to join the fray when the public's health and safety may be in peril because of government inaction? I suspect that it is not enough to reveal the science behind a tragedy like Walkerton and just stop there. There is a duty to ensure that future tragedies are prevented through enactment of laws and/or through education of the public. But there are compelling reasons why this is not the case.

It is risky to confront the government. Particularly if and when research funding comes from the government and dissent is not widespread.

Secondly, it is personally risky. Colleagues, family, spouses and friends may all suffer as bystanders when an individual goes off on a crusade. And the bald fact is that society pays much lip-service to the virtue of whistle-blowing, but privately does not value the individual for this action. And with good reason. There are examples of scientists who have reported wrongdoing, and then, after blowing the whistle, find themselves without a job. Laws have been written to ensure that whistle-blowers do not lose their jobs, but there are many ways of making a job unbearable.

Thirdly, mild constructive criticism from a scientist toward the government is great fodder for the media. The media love to portray the dialogue as a David and Goliath tale. It makes good reading and produces sales. But the portrayal polarizes positions on both sides and ultimately leads to an inability to communicate constructively. The media look for these opportunities.

What should scientists do? If individual scientists are going to get "in the feces", it is best to do it collectively. There is strength in numbers. We need a Canadian scientific forum and voice that is, in essence, a government watchdog and public educator. Its role would be to speak with a collective voice on issues. It would then have the clout of collectivity and would spare the individual scientist the perils of going alone.

# THE DOWNSIDE OF IGNORING NEW SCIENCE

Ironically, there is another side to the coin of the Walkerton disaster. By bowing to the farm lobby and putting off new legislation to deal with manure, the government may well be harming farmers, consumers and the ability to compete in the global market. Manure-management bylaws in sectors of the European Common Market are much stricter than ours. Some sectors already forbid the use of antibiotics in animal feed. Those countries with stricter nutrient management laws cite Canada's lack of proper management as a reason for not importing Canadian farm products. That is already happening.

The cost of new water regulations is high, and the public has never paid the true cost of delivering safe drinking-water. But the cost of a disaster like Walkerton far outweighs the cost of prevention. In the long run, it may well be that governments are better off doing the right thing by enacting timely regulations to protect citizens.

## SUMMARY

It has been a learning experience to observe the government's reaction to a drinking-water disaster — fast science and slow law. It is tricky to tackle the government on scientific issues, particularly if that government sees this as a political threat. In the long run, however, it may be best for government to do the right thing in the first place.

Good scientific communication combined with public pressure may go a long way toward good public policy.

## REFERENCE

McQuigge, M. (2002), "The Walkerton Disaster and Family Physicians", *Canadian Family Physician* (October):1596-1597.

CHAPTER 9

# Science Policy and Public Spending

## J.S.C. McKee

### THE ECONOMIC BENEFITS OF BASIC SCIENTIFIC RESEARCH

This title was the caption to a paper published several years ago by an unlikely pair of authors, a physicist and an economist, and it has played a major role in the assessment of the value of basic research in Britain and elsewhere (Kay and Llewellyn-Smith, 1985). In a real sense it has altered the thinking of political decisionmakers and government bureaucrats because of its emphasis on the funding of fundamental research and discovery as an identifiable investment by society in its economic future.

Christopher Llewellyn-Smith, some time chair of the Department of Physics at Oxford University, and John Kay, Director of the Institute for Fiscal Studies at the same institution, identified general principles that should govern the allocation of public resources to and within science. The thesis that the economic benefits of scientific research are the result of advances in fundamental knowledge is explicit in their paper. They write that:

> The primary reason why we have computers now, and did not have them a hundred years ago is not that we have in the meantime discovered a need for computers, but that we know a great deal more about mathematics and solid state physics than we did a century ago. To equate the useful with the applied is to display the same level of understanding as the child who thinks that the hands are the most important parts of a conventional wristwatch because they are the ones that tell the time (ibid.).

In this context, most scientific research is then an investment by society in its own future success.

However, to postulate that society should specifically support fundamental or basic research on purely economic grounds, as is the case in the paper by Llewellyn-Smith and Kay, is an entirely new concept. The idea that the major justification of basic science is its direct economic return is in many ways revolutionary.

Earlier attempts to justify the public support of basic research have seen the cost of fundamental research as a kind of overhead charge on applied science. J.M. Ziman (1968), A. Weinberg (1967), J.S.C. McKee (1976) and others have tried to ensure funding of both basic science and technology. The direct economic benefit from an investment in basic research was not regarded as quantifiable. Investment in such activity was generally regarded as an act of faith, hope or charity or a mixture of all three.

Kay and Llewellyn-Smith, however, found that making the direct case for the economic value of basic research was so easy that in the end they wonder that it needs to be done. They take as an example the discovery of electricity and its impact on the national income of Britain at a much later date. Assuming a rate of interest equal to the rate of growth, they assess the benefit to the British economy of accelerating the commercial exploitation of electricity by one year as around 5 per cent of annual income or $40 billion (Kay and Llewellyn-Smith, 1985). Indeed, the economic benefit to Britain of advancing the industrial use of electricity by one year exceeds the cost of all fundamental scientific research undertaken in Britain since the time of Newton, an astounding result. But this is not the only quantifiable example.

Inventors of transistors, integrated circuits, nuclear power, electronic industries, induction coils and communications systems owe everything to Thomson, Lorentz, Rutherford, the Curie(s), Faraday, Maxwell and Hertz as fundamental scientists. The huge economic rewards, to society rather than to the discoverers, are transparent. In no instance was such a discovery made in direct response to a perceived need in society.

As we consider these arguments in a local context it becomes clear that scientists should be unequivocal in citing the benefits of basic research to the economy and societal needs of Canada, the United Kingdom or any other country. It may indeed be timely to read a paper by a Canadian physician written twenty years ago entitled "The Cost of Not Doing Medical Research". William Gibson (1980) quantifies the economic benefit to the health-care system inherent in the serendipitous discovery of the polio vaccine, of streptomycin in the treatment of tuberculosis, of penicillin, of insulin and many other materials that have dramatically improved society in the past century. He summarizes his conclusions in one telling sentence, "If you think medical research is expensive, try disease."

The economic benefits of basic scientific research are evident and quantifiable. It is now the responsibility of each of us to ensure that politicians and funding agencies are aware of this fact, and that the base budgets for operating grant support are protected, expanded and seen as a major investment in the economic future of any developed or developing country.

There is much lobbying and educating to be done.

## ARE THERE, OR SHOULD THERE BE, LIMITS TO ECONOMIC GROWTH?

"Exponential growth" is a phrase used to describe the regular increase in a product or quantity when it is characterized by a "doubling time", a constant time interval within which the amount of the substance doubles its previous value. Suppose, for example, I eat one apple on Monday, two on Tuesday, four on Wednesday and eight on Thursday, my appetite for apples is then showing "exponential growth", and there is a doubling time of one day in my habit. This exponential growth, however, cannot under any circumstances be sustained. By Friday the number of apples consumed will be sixteen, and by Saturday thirty-two. Normal bodily functions determine that such growth must level off or decline in the not too distant future and certainly not continue forever. When exponential economic growth is discussed, one thinks of a doubling of certain quantities typical of the economy of a country, and again in a well-defined period of time, not days perhaps, in this case, but years or decades. Is there any real evidence for exponential growth in the economy, and if there is, is this growth of limited duration or likely to continue indefinitely?

I believe that there are several aspects of this economic problem to consider. First, there is population growth which worldwide seems to double in apparently exponential fashion, but which for individual developed countries seems already to be at a standstill. Secondly, there are developing countries whose economic growth in terms of energy consumption per head of the population seems to be increasing exponentially, as poorer countries strive to become industrialized and raise their standard of living to that of their developed neighbours. And, finally, there are countries like Britain, Germany and the United States which have levelled off to the extent that their consumption of energy for industrial purposes is now constant year by year. In the British case, there has been no increase in energy consumption per year per person in the past one hundred years, and Britain was the first modern industrialized country.

Now, if internationally one were to insist as some have suggested, that further economic growth should now be halted and that this planet merely make the best use of what it already has, there would undoubtedly be disastrous political implications for the earth as a whole. There would now be no way in which the aspirations of the developing world could be realized and its standard of living raised to that of its already developed and prosperous partners. For this reason, it seems to me much more appropriate for the developed countries to encourage such countries as Ethiopia and others to adopt the most appropriate means of accomplishing economic growth and financial independence.

Environmentally acceptable and essentially pollution-free energy sources are now available, through solar and nuclear technologies, to do the job. After all, burning of sticks and straw never was, nor can economically ever be, pollution-free on a large scale. And with a rapid improvement in the standard of living of developing countries, through temporary exponential growth in energy demand, they also (if history tells us anything) can reach the constant plateau already reached by Britain a century ago, and in the process while increasing their wealth, solve the difficult problem of overpopulation and arrive at the desired result of constant energy consumption and a stable population.

## HOW GOVERNMENTS RECEIVE SCIENTIFIC ADVICE: A SNAPSHOT!

Twelve years ago, in response to the frustration of scientists seeking funding for research and development projects, I set up a committee to examine science policy in this area. To be specific, I wanted to examine how various governments worldwide received scientific advice, and whether such advice was effective. At that time only 400 out of 50,000 small businesses in Canada had either a scientist or engineer on-board, and university researchers pursuing new knowledge were unable to persuade their funding agencies of the desperate need for support of research and development, innovation and new science.

To tackle this problem and challenge, it was necessary to obtain advice from Canadians in other countries where they had experienced similar problems, and could observe how scientists in those countries felt similar or dissimilar frustrations.

Whereas the data are by now old, and the measurements dated, even now we can appreciate the complexity and diversity of the answers to the question asked. Let me start with Alan Bromley, a Canadian in the unusual position of scientific advisor to the president of the United States, Ronald Reagan, in his last years as president.

When Dr. Bromley received and was responding to my request for information, he was fog-bound in the Baltimore airport. He passed the time helpfully and creatively by dictating a twenty-page letter to me, which I still treasure and it is part of this record. His insights enabled us to relate the responses from eminent physicists in other countries to those from the atypical situation in the United States.

Therefore, to describe the sameness and differences of that time, let me illustrate with a short country-by-country analysis.

In comparing the legislation of science and technology in a variety of developed countries, two highly variable but important parameters arise, one is the status of the political office involved (is it of Cabinet rank?) and the other the size of the budget administered by the minister having science and technology within his portfolio. The following review relates to the year 1990 and thereabouts.

In the Netherlands, the Minister of Education and Science has a large budget and the visibility of the office is high.

In Germany, the Minister for Science and Technology is the third most powerful minister. His budget is large, his effectiveness is evident.

In Japan, the Minister of Education, Science and Culture (Monbusho) has equal status to the Finance Minister. He works closely with the Prime Minister and has a visible office.

In Australia, the Minister for Science has a small budget but good visibility at present due to a common front with the prime minister.

In the United Kingdom, there is no minister in the government responsible solely for science research and development. Science is funded through various ministries and has rather low visibility at present.

In Canada, the Minister of State for Science and Technology is not a member of the Priorities and Planning Committee of Cabinet and his office has a modest budget. Through a new National Advisory Board on Science and Technology and direct access, interaction with the Prime

Minister is more readily achieved than in the case of France. The profile of the office is moderate in Canada. In Canada, however, education is a provincial responsibility, whereas the funding of research and innovation is federal. This reduces the federal involvement in training and education. There is research carried out in twenty-one departments of the federal government, but no minister with overall responsibility. [In December 2003, the Prime Minister appointed a Science Adviser.]

In the United States, no science department of government exists, and no minister of Cabinet rank exists. One wonders how science and technology in that country fare as well as they do, both financially and administratively. Clearly, it is plurality of support that is the secret of scientific success in the United States. Support of science is provided by a substantial number of independent financial agencies. This multiplicity of support systems seems to accomplish in a complex and inertia-fed way what more simple and clear political mechanisms in other countries may fail to produce. The United States is politically and economically different from the other countries under examination.

There is, or was in 1990, no unique way to salvation. But political appreciation of the need for new knowledge and innovation in support of the national economy is now changing the overall economic environment, one country at a time!

## AN ACADEMY OF SCIENCES

When one looks at the ways in which scientific advice can and should be given to government, and the means by which government acquires such advice, past history may not act as a fundamental guide. Indeed, as science issues become more central to the political decision-making process, lack of an appropriate body to provide expert advice on contentious issues becomes increasingly problematic. In Canada, the federal government has been coming under increased pressure to establish a body that draws upon leading-edge scientific knowledge both nationally and globally, and most observers contend that such an initiative should come from outside the political arena.

In Canada, a recent Secretary of State for Science, Research and Development, Dr. Gilbert Normand, came to the realization that Canada needs a National Science Academy to fulfil the role already suggested. He noted, while attending a G8 Science Ministers Meeting, that he was the only delegate without an Academy of Science or equivalent representative in attendance, because no such academy was currently in existence in his country. The campaign to establish a National Academy of Science in Canada began to gain momentum, spurred on by a roundtable convened to discuss options, and the decision to expand the sciences covered by such a body, to include medicine and health. There has been some concern that government should not be leading the consultation process because the Academy might not be seen to be independent. Both government and existing advisory bodies such as the Royal Society of Canada, seem to have reached a working relationship under which a National Academy of Science can co-exist with other existing advisory bodies, of which Canada has a wide variety, ranging from recently created external to government advisory bodies such as the Advisory Council on Science and Technology, and the Council of Science and Technology Advisors, to external committees advising specific government departments. In addition, there are learned societies, policy think-tanks and groups such as the Partnership Group on Science and Engineering that brief the government on behalf of more than twenty national scientific organizations. Since the initial debate on the merits of an Academy of Sciences within Canada, the establishment of such a body has become a key priority in the plan to achieve excellence in the government's agenda. Because the Government of Canada is committed to the country's long tradition of research excellence, a direct link between a strong research base and vibrant economy is well recognized. Knowledge is seen to be the fuel of the new economy, and the driving force to make Canada a global centre for excellence in innovation.

The critical role of knowledge generation and discovery in the economic and social well-being of the country is also acknowledged. As was mentioned earlier, the federal government's science and technology efforts extend over twenty-one departments of government, all of which promote significant research, including the office of the Solicitor General who has the Canadian Security Intelligence Service and the Royal Canadian Mounted Police within his bailiwick.

The then Minister of State for Science, Research and Development, Dr. Rey Paktakhan, in a recent presentation to the Partnership Group for Science and Engineering, emphasized the need for an Academy of Sciences and stated categorically that governments need scientific discovery, and that they therefore need scientific input into making formal policy decisions in areas as diverse as coastal management and genetically modified foods. Such a body could enable government to determine and manage the risks associated with rapid technological development and help politicians make public policy decisions through a credible and independent voice from the scientific community.

The Minister has stated that the scientific community has his full support in the creation of such an Academy. It will be interesting to find out how this idea develops in the coming months and years and whether or not it fulfils the promise that it holds.

As John Maynard Keynes said almost a hundred years ago: "The difficulty lies, not in the new ideas, but in escaping the old ones, which ramify, for those brought up as most of us have been, into every corner of our minds".

## REFERENCES

Gibson, W.C. (1980), "The Cost of Not Doing Medical Research", *Journal of American Medical Association* 244:16.

Kay, J.A. and Llewellyn-Smith, C.H. (1985), "The Economic Benefits of Basic Scientific Research", *Fiscal Studies* 6(3):14.

McKee, J.S.C. (1976), "Death of a Sacred Cow", *Canadian Research* (Nov/Dec):21.

Weinberg, A. (1967), *Reflections on Big Science.* Cambridge, MA: MIT Press.

Ziman, J.M. (1968), *Public Knowledge.* Cambridge: Cambridge University Press.

# PART IV

## SCIENCE, PUBLIC OPINION AND THE MEDIA

CHAPTER 10

# Scientific Evidence, the Media and the Public: The Case of Vaccine Safety Scares

T. Jefferson

## INTRODUCTION

Vaccination programmes, especially those targeting groups such as children, rely on the goodwill of the public. The public (or parents in the case of children) are willing to accept an undefined amount of short-term discomfort (such as fever of short duration or redness at the site of injection) for their children in the near certainty of avoiding the future ills of infectious diseases. This risk-benefit balance is usually not quantified by operators, parents or recipients of the vaccines, but is nevertheless assumed to be acceptable.

Claims of an association between vaccination and the onset of un-expected events appear with regular frequency in the lay and scientific press. The word "association" in the media usually implies that such events are assumed to be a direct and sometimes unforeseen conse-quence of vaccination. For an association to be considered scientific, causality must be proved through a set of epidemiological observations.

New or long-standing serious safety allegations may become threats to vaccination programmes as they may erode goodwill and trust. When this happens the perception of the risk-benefit balance may be affected with a consequent fall in vaccination coverage. This in turn may lead to sporadic cases of the target disease in question or a full-blown epidemic.

A recent example centres around the allegations that MMR (a live attenuated vaccine against three separate important diseases: measles, mumps and rubella) causes rapid onset of bowel disease and autism (autistic entrocolitis) in vaccinated children. The impact of the allegation has been mainly confined to the United Kingdom and other English-speaking developed countries. MMR coverage in the United Kingdom fell to 80 per cent in some areas, while in Ireland even lower coverage led to an epidemic of measles ("MMR Vaccine", 2003).

The scientific controversy, which started soon after publication of a study report, is not over yet and had led to a polarization of both public and scientific opinion between those who believe current evidence proves that an association exists and those who do not (ibid.).

The case of MMR and autism has several features in common with other vaccine safety scares, but many are unique. In the remainder of this paper, I shall examine the nature and role of some of the features and the part played by the scientific media. I shall then try to set out what I think is a reasonable way forward to minimize the risk of future similar events occurring.

## SOME FEATURES OF THE MMR AND AUTISTIC ENTEROCOLITIS STORY

The story broke in 1998 after the publication of a paper authored by a group of researchers at the London teaching hospital, Royal Free, in the highly respected international journal *Lancet*. The paper reported a series of twelve cases (a study design called a case-series) of children who were diagnosed with microscopic changes in the lining of their large bowels and in some cases with autism (Wakefield *et al.*, 1998). The authors reported that ten of the twelve sets of parents had made a connection between prior vaccination with MMR and onset of symptoms. The authors made no such link, merely postulating that the possible onset of autism, a severe childhood disorder of cognitive and behavioural regression may be linked with alterations of bowel absorption (ibid.). A later paper by the same group confirmed the conclusions based on the observation of sixty cases (including the twelve cases from the original series) (Wakefield *et al.*, 2000).

Case-series such as these are commonly used as a possible "danger-signal" generating device and most safety allegations are made by a single researcher or group of researchers.

The unique feature in this case is that the original case-series report did not present the findings as evidence of an association with MMR vaccines; the authors merely stated that a possible association needed further investigation. The association was, however, seriously raised in an accompanying defensive *Lancet* commentary by two highly respected American researchers (Chen and De Stefano, 1998).

Following the publication of the paper in 2000, one of the authors, Dr. Andrew Wakefield, seemed to confirm the presence of an association, going ostensibly beyond what his fellow-authors had agreed. The government of the United Kingdom responded by assembling a panel of experts under the aegis of the Medical Research Council who declared that all the evidence pointed to there not being a link. As the controversy refused to die down and the number of vaccinations being given declined, the government also commissioned a series of studies to further explore the issue. From then on the story took on a life of its own, with extensive coverage in the media. As time went on, polarization between the two camps became evident and led to a war of nerves with a possible early casualty in Dr. Wakefield, who emigrated to the United States.

The long-running nature of the coverage, the consequent scientific and legal battle and the personal nature of the issues are reminiscent of the most controversial vaccine safety scare of the 1970s: that between pertussis vaccines and brain damage. This was finally settled in favour of the vaccine by a court case and series of studies showing no evidence of an association (Griffiths, 1989).

Several of the commissioned MMR studies, mostly carried out by researchers linked to or employed by the British National Health Service, were published in the following years. These rejected the Wakefield hypothesis, while a few studies funded by charities or families' associations had findings confirmatory of those by Wakefield and his associates. As each study was published, the results were hailed by either side as further conclusive proof of absence of a link or a government-sponsored whitewash.

Another key feature of the MMR case was the lack of critical appraisal by both media and scientists of the evidence in the light of methods used by each study.

THE EVIDENCE

Each published study assessing the link between MMR and autistic enterocolitis exhibited fundamental methodological weaknesses. I shall summarize here the content and our methodological assessment of the comparative studies included in our recent systematic review of the evidence (Jefferson, Price, Demicheli and Bianco, 2003).

A case-control study by Davies, Kramarz and Bohlke *et al.* (2001) reported that exposure to MMR was not associated with an increased risk of Crohn's disease and ulcerative colitis. The study had a low chance of bias, but lacked details of exposure, for example, the type of vaccines used, and a discussion of the reference population.

A time-series study by Madsen, Hviid and Vestergaard *et al.* (2002) reported no increased risk of autism or other autistic spectrum disorders between vaccinated and unvaccinated children. The interpretation of this study was made difficult by the unequal length of follow-up for younger cohort members as well as the use of date of diagnosis rather than onset of symptoms for autism.

A single self-controlled case series study by Taylor, Miller, Farrington *et al.* (1999) assessed clustering of cases of autism by post-exposure periods in a cohort of four hundred and ninety-eight (two hundred and ninety-three confirmed cases) children. The authors reported a significant increase of onset of parental concern at six months post-vaccination. The authors argued that this may be due to multiple testing caused by an unclear causal hypothesis and concluded that the evidence did not support an association with autism.

## METHODOLOGICAL PROBLEMS

Each study had a retrospective design, that is, the data used were either already available in some form or other or related to children who had already been vaccinated at the start of the study. This meant that the quality of data, for example, on which vaccines had been used, were not good, as the records had not been primarily intended for research purposes. "Make do with what is already there" in this case was second best as no assessment of association with a particular type of vaccine, batch or manufacturer could be made.

Each study lacked a credible control group, reflecting the universal nature of the vaccination programme. By credible control group, I mean children who had not been vaccinated and who were representative of the group of children who had been. "Representative" controls rule out children of parents who objected to the vaccine or to all vaccines as the families of these children were unlikely to be similar to those of vaccinated children.

Lack of credible controls had two consequences. First, the power of generalizing conclusions, a so-called induction process, of uncontrolled studies was severely limited. Secondly, researchers were forced to use designs such as before-and-after (vaccination) in which the records of the same children were assessed for evidence of autism prior to and post-vaccination. The vaccinated children in essence acted as their own controls.

These designs, although statistically very powerful, are always prone to the interference of known and unknown biases. One of these is bias of attrition (or loss of follow-up) of the study cohort. This bias is present or cannot be excluded when the reasons for losses may be linked to autism or bowel disorder.

Another problem is due to the vagueness of the causal hypothesis. Lack of a defined time frame between vaccination and onset of autism forced the authors of the Taylor study to carry out multiple statistical testing, which is certain to come out on average "positive" in every one in twenty tests. Taken at face value, then, these studies show no evidence of a link. But when appraised critically, their designs and limits show the difficulties of assessing possible unexpected associations of high-coverage, long-running childhood vaccines. Interestingly, none of the studies were published with warnings of their methodological limitations, which calls into question the journals' grasp of the epidemiological and statistical issues raised by these studies. Other studies, which were not included in our systematic review, as we classified them as non-comparative, used even less reliable designs. For example, these included all of the studies reporting evidence of a link, including the original Wakefield case series. Given the potentially huge importance of vaccine safety issues, it is important to identify ways of improving the situation and maximizing our chances of giving scientifically credible and timely answers to future allegations.

## POSSIBLE WAYS FORWARD

Questions on the safety of registered vaccines that have been in use for a while could be answered by using available data or creating the conditions whereby additional data could be made available without huge efforts to mount retrospective studies from scratch. One of the biggest methodological limits of using existing data to answer the autism question is that the original trials (field experiments in which children are assigned more or less at random to either vaccine, placebo or do-nothing) were neither designed nor conducted to address questions on then unknown or unsuspected clinical entities such as autism. They might not have been run for long enough or had designs that were not powerful enough, or the relevant data (e.g., autism) might never have been collected.

Such criticism, however, is only relevant if current practice continues. Currently there is no ethical or funding pressure on researchers to follow-up participants beyond the agreed length of a trial. In addition, records of participants are rarely kept or accessible, so that control or exposed, vaccinated children cannot be identified, say, twenty years after the end of a trial. If instead, these requirements were made universally binding by governments and funding agencies and there was a safe way of keeping records identifying participants by exposure, data could be used to help assess any future causal association hypothesis. Electronic technology for prospective registration of participants and record keeping is available and can be extended to cover routine immunizations carried out beyond the confines of a clinical study.

A further evolution of this concept is that of creating a library of evidence relating to vaccines. Historically, very large amounts of scientific data on the effects of vaccines have been contained in published studies, technical reports, unpublished drafts and the personal files of researchers. Such information is consequently dispersed in a wide variety of locations, including paper libraries, researchers' own homes and institutions' archives. Even when a study is published, space restrictions may mean that not all data are made available. Technical reports of studies (which usually contain more information) are hard to find. Neglect and the passing of time mean that humanity might risk losing important information that could be used again to prevent suffering.

A vaccines library could slow or halt dispersal and loss of such crucial information. Existing studies and knowledge contained in a vaccines library could help clarify and refine study questions and avoid the reinvention of the wheel. If the data were indexed and structured as all libraries do with books and documents, searches could be done and the results made available at relatively short notice.

There is a another spin-off of this idea. The increasing complexity of contemporaneous exposure to several combination vaccines, such as MMR mixed with another antigen, say varicella, makes the assessment of the effects due to a single vaccine progressively more difficult to identify. As no placebo-controlled trials are likely to be conducted on scheduled childhood vaccines ever again, any answer to new questions on the effects of single vaccines or their "basic" combinations must come from a variety of existing sources as well as new studies (if enough good quality data are available). Data are likely then to be a mix of existing and to-be-collected information. Whichever method is chosen, every ounce of knowledge must be extracted from what is collected. Studies on animals can help shed light on effects of vaccines in humans, provided methods are robust. However, animal studies are also widely dispersed; most remain unpublished. Indexing human or animal studies would prevent unnecessary suffering of humans or animals subjected to experiments that have already been carried out elsewhere in the world.

I see a library as a potentially global effort for a number of reasons. Some conditions (such as autism) are so rare that large amounts of data are needed to detect any possible association. These are likely to exceed the capacity of single states. The exponential increase in our biomedical knowledge coupled with its increasing complexity and our growing interest in previously neglected aspects of vaccinology, such as safety, may mean that answers to complex questions will come from a variety of methods, study designs, professional and disciplinary perspectives. Relevance and appropriateness of the evidence must also be assessed by consumers and bio-ethicists.

One last consideration relates to knowledge about vaccines which are no longer produced: the diseases for which they were produced have been eradicated (e.g., small pox), or the "market" is not lucrative (e.g., plague) or too small (e.g., anthrax). Recent bio-terrorist threats have made the maintenance of a knowledge base on such vaccines and their manufacturing processes important, in order to facilitate swifter reactions to future unexpected natural or man-made threats.

If we already have the knowledge, why ignore it?

## REFERENCES

Chen, R.T. and DeStefano, F. (1998), "Vaccine Adverse Events: Causal or Coincidental?" *Lancet* 351:611-612.

Davis, R.L., Kramarz, P. and Bohlke, K. *et al.* (2001), "Measles-Mumps-Rubella and Other Measles-Containing Vaccines Do Not Increase the Risk for Inflammatory Bowel Disease: A Case-Control Study from the Vaccine Safety Datalink Project", *Archives of Pediatrics and Adolescent Medicine* 155(3):354-359.

Griffiths, A.H. (1989), "Permanent Brain Damage and Pertussis Vaccination: Is the End of the Saga in Sight?" *Vaccine* 7:199-210.

Jefferson, T.O., Price, D., Demicheli, V. and Bianco, E. (2003), "Unintended Events Following Immunisation with MMR: A Systematic Review", *Vaccine* 21(25-26):3954-3960.

Madsen, K.M., Hviid, A. and Vestergaard, M. *et al.* (2002), "A Population-Based Study of Measles, Mumps, and Rubella Vaccination and Autism", *New England Journal of Medicine* 347(19):1477-1482.

"MMR Vaccine — How Effective and How Safe?" (2003), *Drugs and Therapeutics Bulletin* 41(4):25-29.

Taylor, B., Miller, E. and Farrington, C.P. *et al.* (1999), "Autism and Measles, Mumps and Rubella Vaccine: No Epidemiological Evidence for a Causal Association", *Lancet* 353:2026-2029.

Wakefield, A.J. *et al.* (1998), "Ileal-Lymphoid-Nodular Hyperplasia, Non-Specific Colitis and Pervasive Developmental Disorder in Children", *Lancet* 351:637-641.

_____ (2000), "Enterocolitis in Children with Developmental Disorders", *American Journal of Gastroenterology* 95: 2285-2295.

CHAPTER 11

# A Question of Trust

## P. Kavanagh

Appearing as a speaker before an audience of specialists can produce a strong feeling of anxiety. This feeling is often calmed by a sensation of trust. Trust that the audience is good intentioned and that communication flows best and works best when there are good intentions and trust on everyone's part.

Trust is one of those complicated, tightly packed concepts that all of us approach differently. And the phrase "whom do you trust?" is fraught with ambiguity. In my family we have a phrase: "I would trust him with my life, but not my money." That could be a comment on the relative priorities of the person in question or a comment on the priorities of the person making the observation.

Trust does not always imply authority or leadership. Trust can be directed or denied to a group, but granted to an individual in that group. Trust can rise and fall depending on the circumstances. The degree of trust accorded may have a direct relationship to how that trust relates to the perceiver's self-interest.

But the key thing about trust is that it is in decline; and this is true everywhere. Almost all forms of authority are under assault: church, government, corporations, schools, academics, police, media, scientists. There is probably not a single aspect of life where the authority figures or authority institutions are not undergoing extreme scrutiny or out-right distrust. It is the age in which we live.

As part of the 2002 Reith Lectures on the BBC, Onora O'Neill spoke on "A Matter of Trust", a follow-up to the Gifford Lectures she gave in Edinburgh in 2001. The talk was a survey of a variety of issues surrounding the idea of trust and it asked questions about why trust is in decline and how it might or might not be improved. O'Neill raises a critical question about the root of the decline of trust. I will sum up her comments as follows: the breaking of a trust, the knowledge that some violation has taken place and the cynicism that this produces is an ever-intensifying and circular effect. The media also plays a significant role in the process of eroding this trust.

On the one hand, I am tempted to suggest that one should not shoot the messenger, on the other, the questions that O'Neill raises about the accountability of the media and its own deceptions, failures and breeches are sobering matters. She also raises very intriguing questions about openness and transparency and whether or not the rush to transparency is a good thing.

One example of this debate came in a story in a recent *Observer* newspaper about experiments in xenotransplants. Appropriately enough it is one of those stories that touches on all aspects of this conference, government, corporations, scientists, law and the media. It is a tale of a court decision that was overturned. The overturning of an injunction which had been issued forbidding the release of documents about experiments in xenotransplants.

Regardless of the merits of the science taking place at the research centre, the circumstances of the story are such that trust will be further eroded. Scientists will be seen as working with corporate interests and with government authorities to engage in practices that were potentially illegal and abhorrent. It goes to the very heart of Onora O'Neill's observations; the bringing to light of the facts of this story through the courts and the media will erode public trust. Unfortunately for all scientists the distrust is not directed solely at individual scientists. The regard for scientists will be diminished. It will be one more instance in the public's mind of scientists ignoring standards, practices, mores and even laws in the "pursuit of truth". In fact, the story dealt extensively with the issues of the media sensationalizing a story and not paying enough attention to the beneficial aspects of experiments. It raised the problem of organ-donor scarcity and the deaths of individuals waiting for organs. It appears a rather fair story in that respect. And that is part of the dilemma; the media's job is to tell the stories of all of us. The truth is that this is a good story. It is about greed, rule breaking, possible animal cruelty and the use of the courts to try and hide the wrongdoing. And thus there is a conundrum.

Part of the difficulty facing the media is that to a certain extent scientists have abandoned the fight to defend animal experimentation, although this experimentation continues. In an article on the organization "People for the Ethical Treatment of Animals" in a recent *New Yorker* magazine, the writer reported that scientists who use animals in their experiments often refuse to talk to the media or to discuss their work. This is an understandable position, as researchers are frequently worried for their own safety. They believe, and with good reason, that if their work gets known, they will be targeted, harassed and possibly physically attacked. But can anyone really suggest that silence and secrecy are the ways to deal with this problem? There are violent, extremist and dangerous forces in society. It is the job of the media to report on them. It is the job of the government and scientists to stand up for what they believe in. And there is reason to believe that being open does not necessarily lead to further declines in trust.

A recent Pew Centre Survey about American attitudes toward science and technology showed that most Americans questioned by the survey saw science as being responsible for the quality of life and future prospects. There is an interesting aspect to this survey. It suggests strongly that those with favourable views of science and technology are actually large consumers of media dealing with science and technology. And those who hold negative views do not pay much attention to the media, they are individuals who form their opinions in other ways. Those who are better educated, according to the survey, consume more media. Therefore, there is an odd situation: the better educated large consumers of media hold positive attitudes toward science; the poorly educated, non-consumers of media hold negative attitudes toward science. What does one make of this? There are several things to conclude. One might feel that better education, more exposure to the media might lead to more positive attitudes toward science and poor education, reduced media consumption might lead to negative attitudes toward science. Where is the issue of trust then?

The rest of the present discussion is about why the media can be trusted and why the media should trust the scientists.

The media can trust that scientists will attempt to communicate out of excitement, pride and a belief that what they have learned is important to the rest of society. The media can also trust that scientists will learn to communicate better and there are ongoing efforts in this area already. The media can trust that scientists will continue to understand to an increasing degree that more and more of what they do is only partly science. It is also politics, business, ethical choices and morality.

There should be trust that scientists know these things, that they understand that they are also citizens of society, and it is critical to play that role. Playing the role of citizens includes participation in the rough and tumble of debate, including those sparked by colleagues.

When the Astronomer Royal argues in his book, *Our Final Century*, that some scientists are engaged in activities that threaten all life, he raises questions that concerned individuals want addressed. Or when a former president of Harvard University raises serious questions about the corporatization of the academy and the corporatization of science, he actually touches the same nerve as the story about animal experimentation. Both Martin Rees (2003) and Derek Bok (2003) are issuing clarion calls that need to be met.

What can one trust about journalists? One can trust that journalists enjoy good stories filled with challenge, character, perseverance and accomplishment. Science has an inherent excitement about it. It is expansive, it pushes boundaries, it opens up the world. All of these elements attract us. When critical public choices and conflicts arise journalists will be there; when scandal, corruption, conflict and struggle are present journalists will be there.

One can trust that the media are not surrogates for education. Their role is informing the world, but not making up for lapses in the education system. In the Pew Survey, mentioned earlier, there is a disconcerting aspect. One of the things the survey does is that it conducts checks on knowledge, on the basis of the opinions. Therefore, it asked what respondents knew of science, in effect, a scientific literacy test. They were simple questions, such as: What is a proton? How far is it to the sun? The results were disconcerting. However, scientific literacy should be the responsibility of the school system rather than the media.

But the media do worry about the literacy of the audiences and not just about the science. A few years ago I was listening to a CBC Radio report on the fiftieth anniversary of the founding of North Atlantic Treaty Organization (NATO). There was a ceremony taking place in Brussels. As I listened, I heard the announcer explaining the origin of NATO. He stated that NATO was formed after World War II and was a coalition of former allies and enemies. The announcer went on to explain that Canada, Britain and the United States had been on one side in the war and Germany had been on the other. I was disturbed by the insinuation that the audience might not know who had been on what side during the war. A colleague in the newsroom explained that fifty years after the fact, part of the audience may not know details about World War II. Trust is a complicated, twisted affair.

There will be a debate about the issues that Derek Bok and Martin Rees raise. Not just because it is possible that journalists as storytellers enjoy conflict. It is the nature of what journalists do. They zero in on conflict, because where there is conflict, there is something at stake, some contesting of values, issues that need further exploration. If Bok and Rees are wrong, say so. Do not trust that by refusing to debate, the issues will not be raised.

Finally, I want to address something that might make the building of trust between the media and scientist possible. It may serve as a building block for trust, a way of seeing similarities between scientists and journalists.

Natural-scientific inquiry is contiguous with other kinds of empirical inquiry. The physicist and the investigative journalist, the X-ray crystallographer and the detective, the astronomer and the ethnomusicologist, etc., all investigate some part or aspect of the same world. And scientists, like detectives, or historians, or anyone who seriously investigates some question, make informed conjectures about the possible explanation of a puzzling phenomenon, check out how well it stands up to the available evidence and any further evidence they can lay hands on, and then use their judgement whether to give it up and try again, modify it, stick with it, or what.

Nor is there any "scientific method" guaranteeing that, at each step, science adds a new truth, eliminates a falsehood, gets closer to the truth, or becomes more empirically adequate. Scientific inquiry is fallible, its progress ragged and uneven. At some times and in some areas, it may stagnate or even regress; and where there is progress, it may be of any of these kinds, or it may be a matter of devising a better instrument, a better computing technique, a better vocabulary, etc.

As human cognitive enterprises go, natural-scientific inquiry has been remarkably successful. But this is not because it relies on a uniquely rational method unavailable to other inquirers; no, scientific inquiry is like other kinds of empirical inquiry—only more so. As Percy Bridgman once put it, "the scientific method, so far as it is a method, is doing one's damnedest with one's mind, no holds barred" (Haack, 2001).

## REFERENCES

Bok, D. (2003), *Universities in the Marketplace: The Commercialization of Higher Education*. Princeton, NJ: Princeton University Press.

Haack, S. (2001), "An Epistemologist in the Bramble-Bush: At the Supreme Court with Mr. Joiner", *Journal of Health Politics, Policy and Law* 26(2):217-248.

O'Neill, O. (2002), "A Question of Trust". The Reith Lecture Series. At <http://www.bbc.co.uk/radio4/reith2002/>.

The Pew Research Center for the People and the Press (2003), "Survey about American Attitudes Towards Science and Technology". At <http://people-press.org/>.

Rees, Sir M. (2003), *Our Final Century: Will the Human Race Survive?* Portsmouth, NH: Heinemann.

CHAPTER 12

# Use it or lose it!

P. Park

This is a story about an opportunity, an opportunity that was almost lost.

At the beginning of April 2003, reports came in on the looting of the Baghdad museum. Pictures of a crying curator being led through the rubble of shattered display cases were being fed *via* satellite around the world. The Discovery Channel programmers decided to interview an archeologist about the artifacts that had disappeared. We wanted to find out what had been lost, why these artifacts were so important, and how they helped to understand the development of western civilization and culture.

The interview was very good, but the scientist's response to the first question was simply a list of missing artifacts. Because it was an interview for use later, we had the luxury of changing it. When the interview was over, some changes were made. Footage of the emotional curator was to run before the interview began; therefore, we started the interview with something along the lines of "How did you feel when you saw the footage from Baghdad, with the broken display cases and toppled statues?" The guest became upset with what he perceived as a silly television question. He did not want to answer such a query. I believe he thought that by responding emotionally to this situation he somehow diminished his credibility. But, in fact, the opposite is true. Good storytellers use emotion. It is one of the tools to help people listen to the story, and more importantly, remember the information. When we explained that his honest response to the pictures could help the audience relate to this important story, the scientist acquiesced. We knew his emotion would be a convincing element to highlight the importance of this story.

When thinking about public opinion and the media, it is important to consider how best to present material to tell the story. The first item to decide is what it is that we want or need to get across to the public.

We have spent too much time trying to figure out how much science people understand, how many facts the public is able to regurgitate, and not enough time trying to help people understand the essence of science, that is, scientific thought and the scientific process. When this essence of science is understood, then individuals can be armed with the information to make knowledgeable decisions.

As Alan Leshner said in his editorial recently in *Science*: "Virtually every major issue facing global society today has science and technology components at its core: terrorism and other forms of violence, economic productivity, health status, climate change and the need for sustainable development" (Leshner, 2003, p. 977). But these are all issues: issues that science is studying, issues for which science frequently has no firm answer, issues that researchers themselves debate using contradictory studies. They can cut to the heart of our deeply held values. In order to form an intelligent opinion of these arguments we must understand the essence of science. Individuals must be able to evaluate differing points of view.

The public must learn to evaluate television programmes like the one that aired on the Fox Network in 2001: "Conspiracy Theory: Did We Land on the Moon?" The thesis of this ratings hit was that the moon landings did not take place. They were staged on a movie set. The film-makers' evidence included the rippling of the American flag as the astronauts planted it into the lunar soil (how could a flag wave in the vacuum of space?). Twenty-five million people saw this programme. It was so popular, Fox re-ran it within a six-month period. A widely used statistic claims that 20 per cent of Americans say Neil Armstrong and Buzz Aldrin never walked on the moon. This conspiracy theory is just one example of why it is important to promote the understanding of scientific thought, the ability to use evidence to form an opinion and use skills to assess that evidence.

In forming opinions on genetic manipulation, stem-cell research or the cost benefits of decreasing carbon emissions, we need to be able to evaluate more subtle debates.

Where do people turn to get their information to form opinions? For the most part they turn to the media, and especially to television.

An April 2002 MORI poll, conducted by the largest independent market research company in the United Kingdom, shows that nine of ten people surveyed stated that they relied on the mass media for at least some of their information about science. Of those polled, 68 per cent cited television news as their main source for information (MORI, 2002).[1] A 2001 National Science Foundation study shows that most adults learn about the latest developments in science and technology primarily from watching television. Forty-four per cent of Americans reported getting their science news from television while only 16 per cent said they relied on newspapers (National Science Foundation, 2002, ch. 7).

Compare that with a study released at the American Association for the Advancement of Science in Denver in 2003. Jon Miller at Northwestern University and Damon Benedict, senior advisor for strategy and planning at the U.S. Department of Energy, presented a poll about science and energy policy leaders. They wanted to know where the policy leaders go for science information. Unlike the general public, they do not rely on television for information about their specialty. In fact, only 3 per cent of the policy leaders cited television, including news and documentaries, as major sources of information about global warming or climate change (Benedict, 2003). They found that the leaders turned to specialty journals, the Internet and even the newspaper for their information. When asked to rate the trustworthiness of the different information sources, both the energy and science policy leaders expressed the lowest level of confidence in the network television reports. They gave these only a three out of ten rating (ibid.). Policy leaders do not rely significantly on television for information to keep up in their specialty, and they do not seem to trust it when they do watch it. This suggests a disturbing chasm between the public and the policy leaders. It is a chasm that contributes to misunderstandings and lost opportunities by scientists and science policy leaders.

I think part of the problem is an arrogance factor about television. "People have been getting too much of their science from television," Craig Venter, co-founder of Celera Genomics Corporation was quoted as saying last year when he accepted his Gairdner Award in Toronto (Abraham, 2002). He was lamenting the lack of public understanding of genetic science, and that too much Hollywood style and not enough facts have left people with misconceptions about the impact of genetics and cloning.

I think that it is time to stop thinking of television as the idiot's plaything and realize that if you want to have an impact on public opinion — use television. If you see something wrong, complain. If a reporter or producer has missed the point, get involved. Television is where people go for their information; therefore, it is time scientists step up to the plate and say, "How can I make it better and how can I use it more effectively?"

Daily Planet, and in its previous incarnation "@discovery.ca", Discovery Channel's flagship show, has tried to help people understand a little more about scientific thinking and scientific studies. It is a science magazine programme that looks at everything from the physics of figure skating to the microbiology of the corona virus. Various interactive initiatives are currently being developed. We have instituted a number of country-wide experiments that will give people an idea of how science is done and even some tips on how to evaluate information.

One experiment that was very successful was the hands-on healing experiment. In conjunction with the University of Toronto botany department, an experiment was set up where bins of tomatoes were injected with a type of tomato blight. There were non-injected control tomatoes kept in the same bins, under the same conditions. The same technician injected and handled the tomatoes. Then a group of hands-on healers were assigned to a particular bin of tomatoes. They were allowed to visit their tomatoes, but not to touch them. Pictures of the tomatoes were put on our Web site and viewers were invited to think healing thoughts about the tomatoes. At the end of the week the tomatoes were uncovered, assessed for the progression of blight and a statistical analysis was done to find out if any of the blighted tomatoes were "healed" by positive thought or hands-on healing. During the week, documentaries were aired about scientists studying various alternative medicine techniques.

The question can be asked: "Why look at hands-on healing?" It is not scientific! On the programme all the problems were discussed: the essence of scientific procedures, setting up an hypothesis, controlling for variables and finding statistically significant results. The topic was fun, and engaging, but was a vehicle for the discussion of more serious scientific requirements.

We must be creative to be engaging, to think of ways to draw the public in; to develop different ways to illustrate unfamiliar concepts.

There is no reason to believe that only one segment of society can understand scientific information. It becomes our failure if we cannot translate, engage and inform effectively. In order to reach out and change public opinion, we need to think about how to use television because that is where most people turn for their information. And that means a number of things.

It means the academic community must make a commitment to reward and recognize the people who take part in television. Shooting a six-minute television story can take more than a day. What kind of support is being provided to the scientists to do this kind of outreach? What recognition is given to those scientists to allow reporters into their laboratories, to those who take time to offer an expert opinion, to those who make themselves and their graduate students available to reporters?

It means scientists must respond quickly to current events. They need to take advantage of what people are discussing, and take the opportunity to talk about something when it is on the public agenda. A Torontonian right now cares about SARS, about viruses, about the spread of infectious disease and the impact of public health on economies. Do you want them to know more about viruses and what makes them different from bacteria, or why having a level-four laboratory in Canada was a great investment? Now would be the time to talk about it because people want to know, and they want to listen, because their health and their livelihoods are on the line. But what about when you want to bring something to the public's attention, what if there are issues that should be in the forefront of the public consciousness? To capture the audience's attention, I believe that science programming needs to be more entertaining — more "Hollywood".

Medicine and health issues are already incorporating the Hollywood element. As Professor Joseph Turow at the Annenburg School for Communication has commented "fictional TV shows reach a much wider audience than most news programmes." He analyzed the content from every hospital-based TV drama on the air during the 2000–2001 season. Shows evaluated included ER, City of Angels, Gideon's Crossing and Strong Medicine. He found that health-care policy issues appeared regularly in the programmes, and that on average, one such issue was dealt with per episode (Turow and Gans, 2002). With shows such as ER attracting twenty to thirty million viewers each week, the study found entertainment television can be more powerful than news in shaping the public's opinion on issues.

How people learn and remember is best done when they are engaged. That is achieved through a narrative structure and with people to whom the audience can relate. This is just what the entertainment industry does best.

The media, especially television, forms and informs public opinion. Scientists must embrace it and learn to speak effectively and directly to the public.

## NOTE

1. Questions were placed on the MORI omnibus, the regular MORI survey among the general public. A nationally representative quota sample of 1,987 adults was interviewed across one hundred and ninety-three constituency-based sampling points throughout Great Britain. Interviews were conducted face to face in respondent's homes between March 7 and 11, 2002.

## REFERENCES

Abraham, C. (2002), "Human Genome Decoder Going Non-Profit: Company Founder to 'Educate the Public' on Ethical Issues", *The Globe and Mail*, April 24, p. A8.

Benedict, D. (2003), "Communication Strategies for Meeting the Information Needs of Science and Energy Policy Leaders". Paper given at the American Association for the Advancement of Science, "Who Leads American Science", February 18, Denver, Colorado.

Leshner, A.I. (2003), "Public Engagement with Science", Editorial, *Science* 299:977.

Market and Opinion Research International (MORI) (2002), "Public Expects the Impossible from Science". At <http://www.mori.com/polls/2002/science.shtml>.

National Science Foundation. Division of Science Resources Statistics (2002), "Science and Technology: Public Attitudes and Public Understanding, Where Americans Get Information about S&T", in *Science and Engineering Indicators*. At <http://www.nsf.gov/sbe/srs/seind02/c7/c7h.htm>.

Turow, J. and Gans, R. (2002), *As Seen on TV: Health Policy Issues in TV's Medical Dramas*. Menlo Park, CA: The Henry J. Kaiser Family Foundation.

# PART V

## RESEARCH, SECURITY AND SECRECY

CHAPTER 13

# The Debate on *The Skeptical Environmentalist* from a Danish Perspective

E.B. Andersen

## INTRODUCTION

It is important to state that the following description of events are intended to be, if not objective, then at least neutral. Secondly, I shall not only report on how *The Skeptical Environmentalist* by Bjørn Lomborg, hereafter called the book, has been received by the international scientific community, but also on its political aspects and consequences, which are more important in Denmark.

Thirdly, I shall toward the end break my intended neutral role and give some reflections on how a national scientific community acts in a situation that obviously extends outside its normal scientific circle; and as such, influences the thinking of scientists and, in fact, forces many to rethink important aspects of their profession.

It is not obvious, or maybe not even necessary, to divide the period I shall try to cover into sub-periods or phases. But it is nonetheless helpful, and I shall do so.

There are three main players on the field in this chain of events: (i) the book itself; (ii) the committee to examine scientific work that does not live up to the unwritten rules for ethical scientific behaviour formed by the Ministry of Science and described in more detail under Phase II; and (iii) the government represented by the Ministers of Science and of the Environment as well as the Prime Minister.

## PHASE I. THE PUBLICATION OF THE BOOK AND ITS RECEPTION

The book was published in Danish in 1998 by a local university press and in an enlarged and revised form by Cambridge University Press in 2001. The Danish version gave rise to much criticism from Danish scientists, especially experts in environmental research, but also by scientists with expertise in the application of mathematical statistics to real data.

As for the second publication in 2001, there was much criticism, some of it rather severe, of the book from leading scientists in the field of environmental research. But, as a contrast, there were also some very positive reviews from serious newspapers and magazines such as the *Washington Post*, the *New York Times* and *The Economist*. Based on the conflicting reviews in January 2002, the *Scientific American* asked four leading experts in the areas covered by the book to give independent reviews and evaluations of the different sections of the book. All four came out with rather strong conclusions to the effect that Bjørn Lomborg has distorted data, has misrepresented the conclusions based on that data, did not take into account the known uncertainty of the data, has cited second-hand data as well-known facts, has been selective and biased in the data used, and has been vague, deliberately or by lack of insight, in statistical methodology (e.g., in his use of such words as "plausible").

Lomborg elegantly rejected the criticism, without going into a real discussion of the basic scientific questions raised by the reviewers chosen by the journal.

## PHASE II. THE COMMITTEE CONCERNING SCIENTIFIC FRAUDULENCE

In 1998, the Ministry of Science proposed in the Danish Parliament to establish (in Danish) *Udvalget vedrørende videnskabelig uredelighed* (UVVU). The Danish word *uredelighed* is hard to translate. The Danish/English dictionary suggests "dishonesty" and "fraudulence". Looking up those words in the English dictionary, I found that the latter definition to be the best. The parliamentary committee passed an act placing scientific fraudulence into law with broad political support.

In February and March 2002, the Ministry of Science received three letters containing very strong accusations of how the book failed to obey even the most simple rules for scientific publications. The Ministry then asked the UVVU (hereafter called the committee) to go into the accusations raised in the letters.

The committee started by discussing whether the book should be classified as science or merely for debate. Some members of the committee voiced the opinion that the book obviously did not live up to the normal requirements for scientific work and hence the letters of accusation should not be a case for the committee to take up. Others felt that even if the book were "bad science", that should not prevent the letters from being assessed by the committee. After lengthy discussions, it was decided to look into the accusations raised by the three letters and to give a verdict as to whether the book was a case of scientific fraud or not.

It was further decided not to involve new reviewers but to base the verdict on a careful reading and discussion of the reviews by the four scientists chosen by the editors of *Scientific American*. It would take up too much space to quote the four reviews. But a few examples may be enough to illustrate how the book was regarded by supposed neutral reviewers.

Most of Bjørn Lomborg's citations are to secondary literature or articles meant for the media.

Bjørn Lomborg uses peer-reviewed papers only if they support his very optimistic viewpoints.

Bjørn Lomborg does not apply a clear distinction between different forms of probability. He uses often the word "plausible", but strange for a statistician, he never gives probabilities for the plausible events.

Bjørn Lomborg's most extreme distortions and worst analyses are his quotations of cost-benefit analyses.

Bjørn Lomborg's book is published by the social science part of the University of Cambridge Press. It is no wonder, therefore, that the reviewers did not detect his unbalanced presentation of the natural sciences. It is a serious error by an otherwise respected publisher that reviewers from the natural sciences were not involved. Lomborg admits: "I am not myself an expert as regards environmental problems." Truer words are not found in the rest of the book (Stephen Schneider).

Bjørn Lomborg uses precise numbers, where there is no foundation for it, and he gives statements based on single citations and without explicit details, as to whether they are representative of the literature.

Lomborg is giving skepticism, and statisticians, a bad name (John P. Holdren).

Bjørn Lomborg's viewpoint, that the number of people is not a problem, is simply wrong. The global growth rate is slowly decreasing, but the growth in absolute terms is close to its highest level observed in the last decade (Jon Bongaarts).

Bjørn Lomborg ignores the significance of biodiversity both as a biological library for science and as an ecosystem service.

The chapter on acid rain is equally badly researched and badly presented. Lomborg states that acid rain has nothing to do with large city pollution, even though it is a fact that nitrogen from traffic is a main source for acid rain (Thomas Lovejoy).

Thomas Lovejoy also points out serious errors in Lomborg's conception of the influence of acid rain on forests.

Based on these four reviews, plus others along with a discussion of whether the book should be regarded as a scientific publication or merely a controversial book, the committee concluded that objectively, the book falls under the category of scientific misconduct. It is clearly a work in clear violation of established norms for proper scientific research. Whether through gross neglect or purposeful fraud cannot or has not been determined.

## PHASE III. THE POLITICAL CONSEQUENCES

It is not a coincidence that the three letters of accusation were sent to the Danish Ministry of Science on February 21, March 7 and March 22, 2002. In January 2002, an institute was formed to advise the Minister of the Environment on matters related to environmental issues, the Institute for Environmental Assessment. To emphasize its independent nature, the institute was to be responsible to a board of scientists and leading persons from the private sector. The board was/is also responsible for selecting the director of the institute. A former professor of political science and now CEO of a large Danish firm was chosen as chairman of the board. (The fact that the chairman had been Bjørn Lomborg's supervisor for his master's dissertation did not receive much media coverage.) At any rate, Lomborg was chosen as the institute's first director on March 1, 2002. It was clearly stated in the three letters that they were sent in response to his selection as director. In the resolution, passed with broad support by the Danish Parliament, it stated very clearly that the director of the new institute should be a person with a broad international reputation as a serious environmental scientist. Therefore, the letter writers were justified in questioning Lomborg's qualifications as specified by the parliamentary resolution; though maybe not the obvious body for the Minister of Science to ask. Nevertheless, it was the committee described in Phase II that was asked to look into the matter.

When the report of the committee was released on January 7, 2003, a veritable storm broke out in the Danish scientific community. First was a number of established professors in the social sciences, who were highly skeptical of the report from the committee. They did not so much criticize Lomborg's book as they criticized the way the committee had handled the case and the foundation upon which they had based their conclusions. One of their claims was that the term "established norms for proper scientific behaviour" as used by the committee in its conclusion, was not the same for the social sciences as for the medical and natural sciences. At the time, three Danish professors took the initiative to collect signatures on a letter to the Minister of Science and the Minister of the Environment containing the critique raised by the social science professors. Of the 13,000 Danish scientists at universities and research institutes, they managed to collect two hundred and eighty-seven signatures. My guess is that many professors did not sign (there are around seven hundred full professors in Denmark) because they knew too little about the book and the surrounding situation.

Lomborg was given ample time in the media, both written and televised, to express his views. In this respect it was helpful that the editor-in-chief of one of three leading newspapers in Denmark openly supported Lomborg and was critical of the committee and its report.

The expected support for the committee and its conclusions followed shortly. A letter formulated by leading professors in medicine and the natural sciences was circulated. It was signed by more than five hundred scientists.

Against all these reactions for and against Lomborg, the government, represented by the Ministers of Science and of the Environment, was under strong pressure to act, either by forcing Lomborg to retire from his position as director of the institute, or by expressing full confidence in Lomborg and his qualifications for the job. The government chose the latter. Thus, the Minister of the Environment and the chairman of the board of the institute both expressed full confidence and continuing support for Lomborg in press releases.

Unfortunately, this did not stop the ongoing debate within the scientific community. So in a rather surprising move, the Prime Minister, Anders Fogh Rasmussen, decided to back up his ministers, and he openly expressed his full confidence in Bjørn Lomborg and his qualifications for running the institute. "The Institute constitutes a refreshingly new angle to the environmental debate; the book is a good book and I have absolute confidence in Bjørn Lomborg" (Prime Minister's Press Release).

## REFLECTIONS

After having read the report of the committee and the articles in Danish newspapers, I am now convinced that the book is bad science, whatever scientific norms are applied.

I believe even the scientists critical of the committee would agree with this viewpoint and that their criticism was directed toward the way the committee had handled the case and formulated its conclusions.

I strongly believe that there is a need for a discussion of the scientific norms for proper research and proper publications in the various disciplines, especially as regards the natural sciences *versus* the social sciences. But the case of Lomborg's book and its reception is not, in my view, the best background for such a discussion.

Three things trouble me. First, the whole matter has divided the Danish scientific community into two groups, which have difficulty coming to terms with each other. Secondly, one often hears laymen, that is, non-scientists, questioning why there is so much quarrelling among the scientists when it is so obvious that Lomborg is right. And thirdly, the discussion in the end became just a political issue.

CHAPTER 14

# SARS: Lessons from the London Pump Handle

R.J. Howard

A story often told in epidemiology is that of the London pump handle and its removal from a local community as a source of drinking, bathing and cooking water in order to control an infectious disease outbreak. It was observed by Dr. John Snow that the outbreak seemed to be most prevalent in a particular part of town that relied on a single source of water for drinking, washing and cooking. Once the handle had been removed, the rate and incidence of disease dropped dramatically, thus proving the link between the water from this source and illness. Essentially, it was the first time in the modern era that a source of origin outbreak had been scientifically and accurately proven, managed and documented in medical literature to show how the spread of disease could be influenced by the use of simple, yet elegant public-health measures, and underscored the dramatic impact that good "shoe-leather epidemiology" could have in controlling the spread of disease. The very symbol of these medical specialists is a worn shoe sole with a hole.

By shoe-leather epidemiology, I refer to the on-the-scene presence of an individual, or a team of trained scientists and medical professionals who understand the principles and practices of effective public-health surveillance, reporting and action. It is hard to imagine a computer or data system that could be programmed to possess the keen powers of observation, scientific intellect, savvy awareness of politics and the cultural, ethnic and medical expertise found in one highly trained epidemiologist.

The past twenty years have been replete with stories of talented, committed physicians and medical experts who have placed their own health and well-being at risk so they could visit the scene of a particularly nasty outbreak simply because they understood the value of having trained eyes on the scene to observe, record and rapidly report findings to competent laboratories and public health-care centres of excellence which could process and report on the results of these specialists. Hanta, Ebola, Lassa and Marburg viruses along with anthrax, plague, Rift Valley Fever, dengue, dracunculiasis and the West Nile virus are all recent examples of how the presence of local, regional and global expertise has come together in order to share knowledge, resources and findings in bringing real science to the scene to determine the cause and possible solutions to disease outbreaks.

At the core of each of these investigations are three principal givens that do not need to be articulated, but serve as the uncompromising basis for solid, effective and honest public health. The rules are that all data would be gathered, collected and shared in a quick, intelligent, scientific manner using targeted and well-designed survey instruments while ensuring the integrity of samples. Secondly, governments would co-operate fully in any investigation; and thirdly, the science would not be compromised, since the findings would make the final determination on the control and prevention of further disease spread. Shoe leather is plentiful in the area of public health, and is always available when called upon in an outbreak of disease.

There appeared to be a problem when SARS (sudden acute respiratory syndrome) first emerged in the Guangdong Province of China as local doctors began to notice the emergence of a particularly virulent strain of respiratory illness in local residents. One can now only speculate how many lives would have been saved in the Far East and Canada had Chinese officials been forthcoming earlier in this epidemic and if they had asked for the assistance of the World Health Organization (WHO) and the Centers for Disease Control (CDC) in the United States. When finally compelled to share the information with sources outside China, mainly because reports were emerging *via* international businesses and cellphone users, Dr. Robert Brieman of the WHO greeted the Chinese delayed co-operation with an understated acknowledgement that "earlier is better" when dealing with disease outbreaks. There was a sense that not all of the information was being shared, even with the most prestigious world health bodies, the WHO and the CDC. These organizations had responded quickly to the 1997 Hong Kong Avian

Influenza outbreak, resulting in the slaughter of millions of chickens in the poultry markets of Hong Kong, and thus averting a pandemic influenza similar to the one in 1918.

Dr. Keiji Fukuda of the Division of Viral Disease, Influenza Branch at the CDC was part of a team, visiting China in February 2003 as part of the WHO team, that initially ventured into the area to examine the outbreak. He was barred from visiting the true epicentre of the illness, and was not allowed to interview doctors or speak to patients. Dr. Fukuda is an expert in this area of medicine at the CDC. His Italian counterpart, Dr. Carlo Urbani, rushed to the scene in late February and is credited with actually identifying the pathogen. On March 29, 2003 he became one of the victims and died after he had spent weeks of around-the-clock technical observation, supervision and efforts to track this deadly and elusive killer. To a great extent, the efforts by Dr. Urbani are responsible for stopping the spread of the disease to other areas such as Vietnam and Cambodia. Again the value of the human factor is seen in the experienced physicians, the quick response, the excellent laboratories and the open dialogue at the scene happening as quickly as possible in a carefully concerted effort to bring in the full weight of the global medical community.

What is clearly demonstrated in the SARS experience is that above all else, there must be the will and desire on the part of governments and elected leaders to do the right thing and move with speed to protect citizens. Global travel, commerce and exploding populations will no doubt present us with other SARS-like "opportunities" to test our skills, awareness and ability to work together, with the same speed as these opportunistic infections move.

Never before has it been as important for elected and appointed officials to fully co-operate with their international colleagues, scientific bodies and global health organizations in combined efforts to stop these new and emerging pathogens. It is vital for senior officials of governments and health agencies to not confuse or replace reassurance with facts. On June 17, 2003, WHO Director General Gro Harlem Brundtland spoke at a scientific conference in Kuala Lumpur and told some 1,000 researchers and health specialists that "SARS has been stopped dead in its tracks". There is little to be gained from this type of scientific hubris and inappropriate reassurance. SARS has neither "gone away" nor been "stopped dead in its tracks". The WHO Deputy General Director, Dr. David Heyman, offered a much more realistic and sobering assessment with his warning "We still don't know if we can stop this disease from becoming endemic". A similar note of caution was issued from the Director of the CDC, Dr. Julie Gerberding, who said, "It is still too early to tell exactly what this virus is going to do. In the meantime, we should exercise caution, make all health professionals and the public aware of the symptoms and report cases quickly".

China has a history of being slow to share with the West those health or scientific findings which, in their minds, would make the Communist Party look bad. From famine to earthquake and dam disasters, to the recent denial of a serious AIDS epidemic, it has been exceedingly difficult to convince the Chinese to be forthcoming with these reports. A Chinese journalist visiting the WHO complained that they were being instructed to play down reports of the illness. That changed finally in early April when the English version of the official *China Daily News* editorially criticized the government and said that harsh reality demands clear information from the authorities, so the public can be fully informed of the situation and take appropriate measures. A subsequent article in the *Asian Wall Street Journal* criticized the Chinese government by saying that they thought first not of the public's health, but of the economic and social harm that might be caused by a panic. The whole world has reason to be angry with China over its mishandling of a new and deadly form of disease that has now spread across the provinces and cities of China, to Asia, Europe and North America.

There is still much to be learned about SARS. While the CDC is firm in its conviction that this is a corona-like virus, there are others who feel SARS or the corona-like virus may just be a collaborator with another pathogen that unites to cause illness and death. But what cannot be questioned is the value of having talented scientific minds evaluating both the epidemiology and the laboratory aspects of this illness as we move toward a definitive finding. These actions are now taking place in laboratories and public health offices in the United States, Canada, China, Great Britain and elsewhere.

Experts have put the economic toll of the SARS outbreak and its mismanagement conservatively at billions of dollars, including cancelled conferences, business ventures, tourism, trade and airline travel. One has to ask, "Could that expense have been reduced had the Chinese government requested the aid and assistance of the variety of global health resources available to them, rather than be silent in an attempt to save face?" In testament to the heroes of this event, the CDC proposed that this new illness be named Urbani SARS-associated virus in honour of the Italian physician who applied his valuable and all important shoe-leather epidemiology to a dangerous and challenging problem which faced the world and lost his life in the process. This is an example of a true medical hero.

In a final, almost ironic note, virtually every serious scientist who studies these emerging viruses predicts that the source of the next virus of this type will likely be China. The combination of over a billion people, poor sanitation, chickens, ducks, pigs and humans create the "viral mixing bowl" of ideal conditions for this to happen. On the outskirts of the very province where SARS began, China has begun construction on a new $1.7 billion airport, China's biggest and most expensive, which will daily carry Chinese citizens around the globe, and citizens of the world to "ground zero" of one of the earth's most complex, natural viral petri dishes. We can only hope for better communications in the future with an eye toward the bottom-line, that being the health of mankind on an ever-shrinking planet.

CHAPTER 15

# The Lessons of Michael Frayn's *Copenhagen*

## P. Calamai

Few contemporary plays have evoked passionate public reaction to equal Michael Frayn's *Copenhagen* which premiered on March 28, 1998 in the intimate Cottesloe Theatre of Britain's Royal National Theatre and has been in production somewhere ever since.

In Ottawa, for example, more than two hundred people turned up at a panel discussion after a matinee performance and stayed for more than two hours. In the United States much of *The New York Review of Books* was given over to impassioned debate about the play's historical basis and ethical dimensions. But all this took place after the subject matter and approach of the play were well known. More revealing about the passion, I feel, is what happened at the Cottesloe on March 27, the last night of previews, when the audience was not conditioned by the opinions of reviewers or other "experts" and was hearing the words, and the underlying ideas, for the first time.

On stage, the Werner Heisenberg character was recounting the horror of attempting to cross a bombed and cratered Germany to see if his family were still alive. As Heisenberg recalled the burning phosphorus sticking to his shoe, an elegant man in his sixties jumped to his feet in the front row of the audience and shouted, "I object. I object to this travesty of history." He continued in this vein for a few moments and then turned on his heel and marched from the theatre. The three actors froze on the stage during the interruption, and then resumed without missing a beat.

Yet even before such passionate audience reactions, before the first reviews, almost all the seats for the initial London run of *Copenhagen* had been sold. What could account for such advance interest:

- The play revolved around Heisenberg and Niels Bohr, two scientists whose names were familiar to many educated non-scientists;
- It was written by Frayn, a playwright with a reputation for "entertaining" fare, even when serious (*Clouds, Noises Off*);
- It featured three prominent actors and a well-regarded director: Sara Kestelman, David Burke, Matthew March, Michael Blakemore;
- The subject matter was the Nazis and the atomic bomb.

Some people find *Copenhagen* a hard slog at first because of "all that physics" and admittedly wave-particle duality is hardly standard theatre fare. But what gives the play its staying power are the themes, which raise ethical and moral questions of universal impact but also of special relevance in today's climate of bioterrorism, human cloning, genetically modified organisms and weapons of mass destruction.

Michael Frayn says the core of his play is the epistemology of intention. The stage Heisenberg ironically suggests the issue may be a "strange new quantum ethics". One commentator opts for a theme of how people respond to evil.

Judging from my experience at the London preview and as moderator of the panel discussion in Ottawa, let me suggest three other aspects of *Copenhagen* which I believe contribute to the chord it has struck in western societies. First, there is a central paradox. The "bad guys", the Nazis, did not kill anyone with an atomic bomb. The "good guys", the Americans, killed at least a hundred thousand non-combatants with bombs dropped on two Japanese cities.

Second comes the issue of where the moral/ethical responsibilities of a scientist lie. Does safety of family come above everything else, or does the survival of the nation or the fate of humanity? Third is a more subtle question, one that lurks just below the play's surface. Where in the chain of discovery of something with the destructive potential of nuclear fission should the ethical dimension first have concerned the scientists involved in "pure" research? (It ought to be trivial that those involved in the Manhattan Project, or Tube Alloys in Canada, had already made their conscious ethical choices.)

Let me deal with this third theme first. Remember that the concept of sustained nuclear fission goes back at least to the early 1930s. In 1934, Leo Szilard, a Hungarian who had fled Germany the year previously, was issued a patent in Britain for an idea he described thusly: "It might be possible to find an element which is split by neutrons; thus when such an element is assembled in sufficiently large mass, a nuclear chain reaction can occur." At Szilard's request, the British Admiralty classed the patent as secret. Did the ethical clock begin to tick then?

Or should it have started on December 24, 1938. That is when Lise Meitner was hiking with her nephew, Otto Frisch, outside Stockholm. They discussed a letter that Meitner, a Jew who had been forced to flee Germany, had received three days earlier from Otto Hahn, her long-time collaborator in Berlin. Hahn reported that their experiment of bombarding uranium with neutrons had produced barium, a result he could not explain. But Meitner and Frisch realized that the uranium nucleus had split into two new nuclei, theoretically releasing about 200 Mev in the process. Do you hear a ticking yet?

Maybe you prefer January 13, 1939 as the start date for the ethical countdown. After all, that was the day that Frisch carried out the uranium-barium experiment at the Niels Bohrs laboratory in Copenhagen and confirmed the projected release of energy. Bohr had already gone to the United States and had talked about Meitner and Frisch's work in Princeton and at an American Physical Society meeting in Washington, DC. Within days, U.S. scientists had confirmed the fission results.

Surely by this point, physicists should have been raising the question of whether it was ethical for them to continue in this line of research without a public examination of the potential consequences. As numerous historical accounts make clear, what happened instead was that Szilard and Edward Teller went to see Albert Einstein, who then wrote President Roosevelt that this research opened the way to a weapon of mass destruction and that the United States had better get cracking. If they had any ethical qualms, prominent American physicists had managed to put them aside as they lined up for a new source of funding for their pet experiments. Ernest Lawrence was one of the most adroit, as author Gregg Herken clearly documents in his book *Brotherhood of the Bomb* (Herken, 2002).

This brings us to the second of my ethical markers; where do a scientist's prime loyalties lie? This is a question that Frayn explores powerfully in the play, with the stage Heisenberg torn between the fear that the Allies might develop an atomic bomb and annihilate his family, friends, even much of the Germany he loves. On the other hand, to put a weapon of such destructive power in the hands of an obvious paranoid psychotic like Hitler could endanger the entire world. How Heisenberg resolved this dilemma is still disputed among historians, although Frayn's play has brought to light previously unpublished contemporary written accounts from some of the principals. In Heisenberg's *post-hoc* accounts, it seems clear that he thought that he was subtly suggesting to Bohr that Germany was working on a bomb, but that there was still time for physicists on both sides to agree not to work on nuclear fission during the war. When this approach failed, one school of thought suggests that Heisenberg deliberately steered the German bomb effort into a blind alley. Another argues that he did so inadvertently, by grossly miscalculating the amount of $U_{235}$ needed for a bomb. There is a tendency among those historians holding the latter view to be very grudging in acknowledging that any prominent German actively strove to undermine the Nazi regime.

We know what happened on the allied side. The best physicists in Britain, Canada and the United States lined up to help build the bomb. Bohr also managed to get to Los Alamos toward the end of the project, but his direct contribution appears to have been minimal. Herken quotes Teller saying that Bohr's design for a bomb trigger was hopelessly impractical. At the eleventh hour, when the bomb was ready to be dropped, a group of prominent physicists, including Lawrence and Enrico Fermi, argued for a demonstration on a desert or barren island before official United Nations observers. Leo Szilard also circulated a petition urging that the atomic bomb not be used against Japan without warning. But these ethical chimes were not heard in some quarters. When Robert Oppenheimer read Szilard's petition, he told Teller that it was not the job of scientists to decide how the weapon was to be used. Teller also refused to sign the petition, setting out his views to his fellow Hungarian in a letter with these prophetic words:

> The things we are working on are so terrible that no amount of protesting or fiddling with politics will save our souls ... I should like to have the advice of all of you whether you think it is a crime to continue to work. But I feel that I should do the wrong thing if I tried to say how to tie the little toe of the ghost to the bottle from which we had just helped it escape (Herken, 2002, p. 135).

And this brings us to the paradox which I proposed as the first of the three aspects that cause the play to resonate with audiences. The Nazis did not kill anyone with an atomic bomb. The Americans killed hundreds of thousands. Yet as the fictional Heisenberg points out, he will always be remembered as a physicist willing to research a means of mass murder while Bohr will be recalled as the avuncular theoretical physicist. And that is only just, Heisenberg says in the play, because we do take people's intentions into account when passing moral judgements on them. And we ought to. Not to do so would require some "strange new quantum ethics". When you see the play it is obvious that Heisenberg is engaging in irony with this line of thought. The British audience mostly got it. Many of the American academic critics failed to.

Before too much Canadian smugness sneaks into this account, perhaps I should note that Canada's most prominent scientist was also a very willing handmaiden of research to kill as many Germans as possible, as chronicled by author-journalist John Bryden, a member of Parliament, in his book *Deadly Allies* (Bryden, 1989). On a clear fall afternoon in 1940, Sir Frederick Banting and three colleagues watched from boats on Balsam Lake in the Kiwarthas as a low-flying airplane loosed plume after plume of sawdust across the waters. This was the first Canadian field experiment in germ warfare, with the famous co-discoverer of insulin measuring how sawdust, soaked in the highly contagious parrot fever virus, could be used to rain death from the sky onto the German enemy if they dared resort to germ warfare. An excited Banting wrote in his diary afterwards about the prospect of retaliating by killing "3 or 4 million young Huns ... without mercy ... without feeling" (Bryden, 1989).

The ethical issues surrounding scientific research in the service of war are obviously not confined to the stage or to history. The world has just seen an overwhelmingly powerful state invade and conquer a weak, impoverished country with the justification that scientists there had developed weapons of mass destruction. Yet none of these weapons were deployed in the one instance where you might most have expected their use: to protect the state from invasion. And none of them have yet been found.

In Canada, we should also have real and current ethical questions about the military application of scientific research. The federal government has recently negotiated access for Canadian university researchers to MURI, the Multidisciplinary Research Program of the University Research Initiative of the U.S. Department of Defense. This programme makes awards to researchers, typically U.S.$1 million a year for up to five years, on behalf of four Department of Defense research offices: Army, Navy, Airforce and Defense Advanced Research Projects Agency (DARPA). Projects for 2003 included:

- Active-Vision for Control of Agile Manoeuvring Aerial Vehicles in Complex 3-D Environments.
- Integrated Artificial Muscle, High-Life Bio-Hydrodynamic and Neuro-Control for Biorobiotic Autonomous Undersea Vehicles.
- Direct Nanoscale Conversion of Biomolecular Signals into Electronic Information.

Is this really research that Canadians want their government to be facilitating? Has anyone raised publicly the question of where in the chain of discovery such research is located. It does not take much imagination to see what use the U.S. Air Force would make of an Agile Manoeuvring Aerial Vehicle. Or why the Navy might be pursuing sophisticated control for Biorobiotic Autonomous Undersea Vehicles.

Perhaps we are simply hoping that because our intentions are not evil, Canadians will be seen as the "good guys". Michael Frayn's *Copenhagen* demonstrates that such hopes are little better than self-delusion.

## REFERENCES

Bryden, J. (1989), *Deadly Allies: Canada's Secret War 1937-1947*. Toronto: McClelland & Stewart.

Herken, G. (2002), *Brotherhood of the Bomb: The Tangled Lives and Loyalties of Robert Oppenheimer, Ernest Lawrence and Edward Teller*. New York: Henry Holt and Company.

# PART VI

ETHICS

CHAPTER 16

# Professionalism: A Vehicle for Scientific Responsibility?

## H.B. Dinsdale

### INTRODUCTION

Science and technology are major forces that can lead to rapid change in the social and natural environment. Science therefore carries serious responsibility. Scientists have been accused of often showing insensitivity to the ethical implications of their work. Are scientists behaving responsibly?

I will examine responsibility in science from the perspective provided by the concept of professionalism. My comments derive from my familiarity with medicine, but they can be applied to all professions.

### THE ORIGINS OF PROFESSIONALISM

The roots of professionalism are found in the craft guilds of the Middle Ages. Guilds were formed to oversee and regulate the activities of all practitioners of a given craft in a region, usually controlled by a town. Guilds had an economic motive combined with juridical, political, social and at times religious aspirations (Krause, 1996).

Guild authority included the following four important dimensions: (i) power and control over the association, (ii) the workplace, (iii) the market, and (iv) the relation to the state. The earliest guilds had the power of association granted to them by the feudal lord, thereby enabling them to be the main method of organizing work. The principle of self-organization and self-government of the group by the group, a *universitas* in mediaeval Latin, provided the power to create an association of equals. This principle of self-rule was described as the "ascending principle", in contrast to the "descending order" of rule by princes and feudal lords. The descending principle usually prevailed in the countryside, the guild order in the towns.

The association determined the length of apprenticeship required in each guild and prescribed the behaviour expected of each journeyman who had completed an apprenticeship, but was not yet accepted by the guild as a master. The guild courts assessed fines and sanctioned or expelled masters. The rights and obligations of the guild rested with the masters, who were required to be equals and colleagues. Guild masters had control over the workplace because they owned the tools and the workshop. Masters deliberately limited production in order not to debase the quality of the work.

The third power, control over the market, derived from the guild's monopoly over the product made or the skill provided. That monopoly had to be granted, leading to the fourth power, the relationship between the guild and the state. Power over that relationship varied from one country to the next. The less centralized the state government, the greater the power of the guilds.

Craft guilds gradually declined in power, but the Middle Ages saw the rise of the scholars' guild, the university, which survives to the present day. The prototype of the university guild in Bologna was created by the masters in response to the formation of a students' guild. The masters gradually took control over the students, a circumstance periodically contested!

By the early Renaissance, physicians and lawyers had begun to develop their own practitioners' guilds. They interacted with scholars' guilds so that scholarly education was followed by an apprenticeship period with established community professionals. England differed from the continent in that professional associations developed outside the university. This historical lack of powerful alliances with professional groups, it has been suggested, may have made "arts and sciences" universities in England more vulnerable to attacks by the state (Kogan and Kogan, 1983).

## THREATS TO PROFESSIONALISM

Early social science literature on professionalism considered its benefits to outweigh its disadvantages because of its commitment to service (Parsons, 1939). However, the literature began to change in the 1950s;

the expectation that professions would demonstrate both altruistic and self-interested behaviour was considered a contradiction (Durkheim, 1957).

During the twentieth century, the state became an increasingly important factor affecting professional life. Marxism attempted to proletarianize the medical profession. Many western governments created large bureaucracies to deliver publicly funded health care. In addition to the state, medicine was impacted by capitalism, exemplified in the United States by health maintenance organizations that ration care and impose gag orders on physicians. The industrialization of clinical research is another example of the imposition of corporate interests (Dinsdale, 2002). As Richard and Sylvia Cruess have commented, "it is interesting that very few of the sociologists, economists and political scientists who have analyzed corporate and bureaucratic influences in medicine have offered solutions to the problems posed to the individual professional by the dilemmas they have identified" (Cruess and Cruess, 1997).

The current threat to professionalism in the United States was summarized by Wynia and colleagues in the *New England Journal of Medicine*: "The role of professionalism has been so little discussed that it has virtually disappeared in the battle between those who favor market competition in a trillion-dollar industry and those who seek greater government regulation" (Wynia, Latham, Kao, Berg and Emanuel, 1999).

## PROFESSIONAL RESPONSIBILITIES

What responsibilities flow from calling yourself a professional?

The current *Oxford English Dictionary* defines "profession" as "an occupation, especially one that involves prolonged training and a formal qualification". A key omission in that definition is the contract with society on which professionalism is based. That contract, which began with the guilds, requires public trust. That trust depends in turn on the integrity of individual professionals and their profession as a whole.

Three fundamental principles characterize medicine's social contract: (i) the primacy of patients' welfare, (ii) patient autonomy and (iii) social justice. If those principles are maintained in the face of pressures from the state and capitalism, then professions, in this case medicine, are indeed trustees of the public interest (Philips, 2001).

Furthermore, the service that a professional provides for the common good can enhance society through aesthetic or other means. An architect can design a safe and efficient building. But truly professional architects will also wish to add beauty and elegance to their work.

Professions protect not only vulnerable persons but also vulnerable social values. Illness limits the ability to shop around when important decisions have to be made. Professional groups, through the establishment of standards, continuous education and peer review can do much to supply quality assurance. If not, public criticism will ensue, such as characterizing physicians as servants of the state or tools of business.

Professional self-regulation has come under increasing scrutiny and its legitimacy challenged, a reflection of the wider challenge to authority at large in society. Egregious corporate scandals such as Enron's collapse in the United States and the serious professional misconduct of two pediatric cardiac surgeons in Bristol, U.K. cause outbursts of public anger. This paper may or may not lead to regulatory and professional reforms. Professions must exercise the responsibility of self-regulation and must define and organize educational and standard-setting processes for current and future members.

A balance must be maintained between internal and external accountability. Governments view efficiency, effectiveness and measured outcomes of professions as the best way to judge their services. However, regulatory agendas may reflect politics, history and even chance rather than priorities identified by professionals. Commentators have suggested that in the United Kingdom the professions have tended to allow the discourse to be conducted by the government on its own (McGettrick, 2003). That is probably also the case elsewhere.

The alternatives to professional power are capitalist power, state power or some combination. It is important for professionals to understand the context in which self-regulation may continue. The current context, derivative from the guilds, involves legislation, regulation and accreditation. *Legislation* is the law, considered collectively. Laws are the system of values which, in a particular country or community, regulate the action of its members and which may be enforced by the imposition of penalties. Elected representatives pass laws in a democracy. *Regulations* are rules or directives made and maintained by an authority. They are the mechanism by which government bureaucracy implements legislation. *Accreditation* is a self-assessment and external peer assessment process used by professional organizations to accurately assess their level of performance in relation to established standards and implement ways to continuously improve. Professions must identify the need, develop and maintain credible procedures of accreditation and establish rules of conduct.

My comments up to this point relate mainly to the profession of medicine and biomedical research. What are the social contract, rules of conduct and assurance mechanisms that have been developed by non-medical professions, scientific or otherwise?

The American Mathematical Society Ethical Guidelines are organized under the topics of mathematical research and its presentation, social responsibility of mathematicians, education and granting of degrees and publication. The section on social responsibility deals with confidentiality, avoidance of bias and conflicts of interest, and disclosing implications of their work to the public (American Mathematical Society, 1995).

The Chemist's Code of Conduct states that chemists have a responsibility to the public, the science of chemistry, the profession, the employer, employees, students, associates, clients and the environment (American Chemical Society, 2003).

The British National Union of Journalists has a twelve-point Code of Conduct that deals mainly with the credibility and handling of information (British National Union of Journalists, 1994).

Others can assess whether or not mechanisms are in place to ensure that such guidelines and codes are observed. The public will support science only if it can trust the scientists and the institutions that conduct research. Pseudo-accountability and scientific misconduct have far-reaching consequences.

## SCIENCE: BROADER RESPONSIBILTIES

Western governments place a priority on supporting research that can be translated into economic benefits. What happens when laws of the market-place overtake traditional norms and values of science? One consequence is that the benefits of science are spread unevenly around the globe. Indeed, much of the investment in science in the last 75 years has been motivated by wars.

Scientists should be committed to finding solutions for today's most pressing problems. However, the consequences of research are virtually impossible to foresee. The scientific community must recognize the potential for such consequences and be prepared to address the questions they create.

The public does not conceive of science as a voice for them. That role has been largely taken over by non-governmental organizations and special interest groups. But there have been voices of scientific responsibility. The Pugwash Conferences on Science and World affairs, an initiative of Bertrand Russell and Albert Einstein, supported by Cyrus Eaton, a Canadian industrialist, provide a forum for distinguished scientists such as Eugene Rabinowitch, a biophysicist, who was involved in the nuclear issue. He was the author of the report of the 1961 Pugwash Conference. The substantive opening paragraph of that report states:

> Science misused by nations to foster their competitive interests as world powers makes possible the destruction of mankind. Science used cooperatively by all nations for the increase of knowledge and the improvement of man's productive capacity can give all men on earth a satisfactory and worthwhile life. Scientists bear a responsibility both to foster the constructive use of science and to help in preventing its destructive use (Rotblat, 1972).

Would that statement today be considered hopelessly naïve? Hopefully not. Revisiting professionalism and understanding its social contract would provide science an important foundation for individual and collective responsibility.

## REFERENCES

American Chemical Society (2003), "The Chemist's Code of Conduct". At <www.chemistry.org/portal/chemistry>.

American Mathematical Society (1995), "American Mathematical Society Ethical Guidelines", adopted March 18. At <www.ams.org/secretary/ethics.html>.

British National Union of Journalists (1994), "Code of Conduct", adopted June 29. At <www.uta.fi/ethicnet/uk.html>.

Cruess, R.L. and Cruess, S.R. (1997), "Teaching Medicine as a Profession in the Service of Healing", *Academic Medicine* 72:941-952.

Dinsdale, H. B. (2002), "The Framing of Decisions: The Clinical Trial", in *Statistics, Science and Public Policy VI. Science and Responsibility*, ed. A.M. Herzberg and R.W. Oldford. Kingston, ON: Queen's University, pp. 147-155.

Durkheim, E. (1957), *Professional Ethics and Civic Morals*, translated by C. Brookfield. London: Routledge and Kegan Paul.

Kogan, M. and Kogan, D. (1983), *Universities Under Attack.* London: Kogan Page.

Krause, E.A. (1996), *Death of the Guilds.* New Haven: Yale University Press.

Parsons, T. (1939), "The Professions and Social Structure", *Social Forum* 17:457-467.

McGettrick, B. (2003), "The Professions: Grounds for Hope in Scotland", *Journal of the Royal Society of Arts*, February.

Philips, M. (2001), "The Professions Must Resist Being Blair's Scapegoats", *The Sunday Times,* March 11, p. 6.

Rotblat, J. (1972), *Scientists in the Quest for Peace: A History of the Pugwash Conferences*. Cambridge, MA: MIT Press.

Wynia, M. K., Latham, S.R., Kao, A.C., Berg, J.W. and Emanuel, L.L. (1999), "Medical Professionalism in Society", *New England Journal of Medicine* 341:1611-1616.

CHAPTER 17

# The Missing Snake

A.F. Merry

Traditionally, the surgeon was the "captain of the ship". A surgical decision was founded on the notion of authority: the extensive training, high qualifications, hard-won experience and senior position of the surgeon justified the authority to make decisions about patients. Actions were judged against the standard of the reasonable doctor. This legal position was encapsulated in the Bolam principle of 1957 (Merry and McCall Smith, 2001). On this principle, there could be no finding of negligence provided a doctor acted in accordance with "a practice accepted as proper by a responsible body of medical men skilled in that particular art". Negligence would not be inferred merely because there was a body of medical opinion that took a contrary view. Scientific evidence was secondary to authoritative opinion and perceptions of accepted practice. Patients were seen as belonging to the surgeon, and largely expected to do as they were told.

Attitudes have changed. Informed consent has become much more important in decision-making. Since the pivotal 1992 Australian judgement in *Rogers v. Whittaker* (Merry and McCall Smith, 2001), practice has been judged against the standard of the reasonable patient. Furthermore, it now seems likely that the reasonable patient will expect so-called evidence-based medicine. Patients are seen as autonomous and therefore entitled to make their own decisions. To do this, they need to know what the best available evidence shows. Surgical decision-making today depends upon the ability to provide this information. Training and experience are still important, but so is a thorough and up-to-date grasp of the medical literature.

Levels of evidence have been identified. Typically, the highest level involves evidence from at least one well-designed randomized controlled trial, or preferably evidence from systematic reviews with meta-analyses of the data from multiple randomized controlled trials. The lowest level of evidence is assigned to the "opinions of respected authorities, based on clinical experience, descriptive studies or reports of expert committees" (Douketis, Feightner, Attia and Feldman, 1999). This approach has limitations. Some questions do not easily lend themselves to a randomized controlled trial. A rather obvious example would relate to parachutes used by individuals when jumping out of an aeroplane: there is in fact no evidence from randomized trials to support the use of this technology, but most people would be guided by first principles (supported by anecdote) in this situation. In this example there is, of course, a clear causal link between survival and parachute use, and death and parachute failure. There are aspects of medical practice for which the links are similarly self-evident. However, it is more common for the underlying causal mechanisms to be unclear, and in these circumstances large randomized controlled trials are often the best guide to decision-making. Unfortunately, evidence of this type is not always available. A great deal of practice that is accepted as good medicine today is still not supported by anything more than expert opinion, based on experience. Furthermore, surgeons are often faced with situations in which time for contemplation and opportunity for consultation is limited. In consequence, there is major variation in practice, even between highly reputable practitioners, as well as in respect of elective procedures.

It is sometimes suggested that variation in general is simply evidence of the pursuit of excellence. By this argument, progress depends on pushing the limits and extending the boundaries of practice. Innovation and change are seen as essential for improvement. It is true that most surgeons change the fine detail of their technique from operation to operation, particularly when learning a new technique. This is part of developing their skill and expertise. Even after a technique is established in the hands of a particular surgeon, situations may well arise when some modification of the standard approach seems warranted under the circumstances. It would certainly be wrong to insist that a surgeon be constrained from responding in the best way to the unique challenges presented by each individual patient. Furthermore, modifications in an individual case may lead to new and better ways of doing the procedure in future cases. Unfortunately, however, the justification for variation is often not at all clear. For example, the rate at which certain procedures are undertaken (notably hysterectomy, but also coronary grafting, the insertion of grommets and many other examples) differs five-fold or more between centres, even though the mix of patients and resources is indistinguishable. While one may not be sure whether the optimum lies at the upper rate, or the lower, or somewhere in between, one is probably safe in surmising that the entire range is unlikely to be appropriate.

How does the modern surgeon reconcile these conflicting tensions in an ethical manner? At what point does one say that a surgical decision has crossed the line between acceptable variation in practice and unacceptable experimentation? How should the law view surgical decision-making in the absence of clear evidence on what ought to be done? To understand the present it is sometimes helpful to reflect on the past. In doing so, the value of mythology and its symbolism should not be overlooked.

Medicine and the law are each identified strongly with a symbol. For the law, this symbol is a set of scales, typically shown in the left hand of Themis, the Greek goddess of justice (called Justitia by the Romans). They represent fairness and balance. The Lady of Justice is usually depicted as also holding a sword in her right hand; the sword is a symbol of enforcement. Today she is almost always depicted as blindfolded, but the blindfold was only added in the sixteenth or seventeenth century. There are two views on its significance. One is a positive view: that the blindfold represents impartiality. The other view is more cynical: it suggests that the blindfold was added to indicate that the courts could not see what was in front of their noses and that justice was indeed blind. This view may reflect a difference in perspective rather than absolute blindness on the part of the courts, but doctors should take note.

It is received wisdom that the symbol "properly" representing medicine consists of a (single) snake, coiled around a staff. The snake is *Coluber longissimus,* also called *Coluber aesculapii.* Harmless, and typically about four feet long, this is one of two snakes widely seen throughout Europe. It climbs well and can swim. Although savage when first caught, most members of the species become tame and like being handled by familiar people, although not by strangers (Boulenger, 1913). The staff belongs to Asclepius (Aesculapius to the Romans). The legend of Asclepius may derive from a real person, a great physician who lived in about 1200 BC. The symbolism of the snake is obscure, with various explanations of which most are implausibly prosaic. Serpents hold a pre-eminent position in the individual and collective subconscious of mankind (Wilson, 1998); therefore their place in this symbol is not surprising. Neither is it surprising that, in the legend, Asclepius appeared, at times, in the form of a snake. In legend, he acquired a substantial knowledge of surgery, and also of pharmacology. Foremost in his pharmacopoeia was a potion from Athena, derived from the blood of a gorgon. If the blood was taken from the left of the gorgon, it was poisonous, but if taken from the right it had miraculous healing properties. So powerful were these latter properties that Asclepius succeeded in raising the dead. It is not necessarily advisable today for a physician to become too successful, nor was it then; Zeus took objection to this mortal's overstepping the mark, and dispatched Asclepius with a thunderbolt. However, the cult of Asclepius survived and for centuries ill people were tended in *Asclepieia,* places of refuge populated with tame snakes. Hippocrates (460 – 377 BC), the father of modern medicine, was a twentieth-generation member of the cult of Asclepius, and trained in the Asclepium of Cos.

Hippocrates replaced superstition with an emphasis on the physical and the rational. He may therefore be said to have begun the tradition of evidence-based medicine. He was a skilled practitioner, but he could also be described as a medical innovator. Subsequent innovations in medicine included: Andreas Vesalius' publication of the first scientifically based anatomy textbook, *De Humani Corporis Fabrica* in 1543, William Harvey's discovery of the circulation of blood, described in *De Motu Cordis* in 1628, and Joseph Priestly's discovery of oxygen (with Carl Scheele) in 1771. On the basis of this rapid increase in scientific knowledge, surgery developed. Science was in the ascendancy and the need for snakes was in retreat, but progress was inhibited by two major barriers. One of these barriers was microbiological. Surgeons dressed in frock coats for their operations and kept the handles of their scalpels clean, but they often failed to wipe the blades between patients. Until Lister introduced the concept of asepsis in 1867, infection was rife and was responsible for the demise of many patients who might otherwise have been cured. The other barrier was pain: the almost unbearable pain that dominated these procedures limited what could be done and made speed the greatest virtue a surgeon could possess.

On October 16, 1846, with a newly invented and constructed vaporizer, William T. Morton anesthetized Edward Gilbert Abbott while J.C. Warren ligated a congenital venous malformation in his neck. Morton had arrived late, and it is to Warren's enormous credit that he waited for him. In doing so he added considerable loss of face to the risk he was already taking in permitting a relatively unknown practitioner the opportunity to carry out an experiment thought very likely to fail (Fenster, 2001). However, Warren was committed to the experiment. This was innovative practice in action, and it was successful innovation. At the end of the procedure, Warren turned to the assembled audience and said "Gentlemen, this is no humbug". Like parachuting, anaesthesia met the "between the eyes" statistical test (i.e., the effect was so obvious that it hit the observer between the eyes). It self-evidently worked and no randomized controlled trial was necessary. This discovery (with Lister's) changed the progress of surgical practice, and initiated an exponential increase in technical and clinical knowledge that is still accelerating.

It is no exaggeration to say that the discovery of anaesthesia changed the lot of humanity. It is therefore interesting to reflect that Asclepius lived (or is reputed to have lived) 3,200 years ago and Hippocrates 2,400 years ago, but anaesthesia has been with us for only slightly more than one hundred and fifty years. It is, furthermore, salutary to reflect that this extraordinary advance was not ushered in under the auspices of ethical decision-making. No ethics committee met to approve the planned experiment. It is not clear to what extent the patient was informed about the risks, although it is certainly obvious, in hindsight, that they were substantial (the first recorded death from anaesthesia occurred little more than a year later). There is a strong sense that the decision to use anaesthesia was made on the basis of authority; it was innovative practice driven by Morton's pursuit of fame and fortune and Warren's preoccupation with the problem of pain. We are indebted to them both, beyond measure, but today we might question the ethics of their approach.

A wide-spread acceptance of a role for this type of informal experimentation in medicine persisted until quite recently. As a young trainee in anaesthetics, I was told that anaesthesia provided a perfect physiological and pharmacological model for experimentation — my teachers advocated doing something different every day. The idea was that trial and error would hone our expertise and advance the practice of anaesthesia at the same time. Patients, it was assumed, would be grateful for our commitment to progress. To be clear, it was understood that there were limits: nothing too risky was permitted, and experimentation was confined to areas where correct practice was unclear. Often it amounted to no more than choosing one of two established techniques on one day and the alternative on the next, but this choice was held to be in the domain of the practitioner rather than that of the patient. This approach was informal and unstructured, and almost always ineffectual in advancing knowledge. It served to promote decision-making on the basis of anecdote, and tended to cement the notion of authority, based on training and experience, as the key to good practice.

A somewhat similar approach to the management of cervical cancer was being followed at that time by Professor Herbert Green at Auckland's main centre of gynaecological surgery. Professor Green believed that too many hysterectomies were undertaken (and there was good reason for this belief). He further believed that early signs of cancer detected on cervical screening would not necessarily progress. He therefore adopted a conservative approach to the management of low-grade abnormalities on cervical smears, but did not include his patients in this decision. Sandra Coney, an investigative journalist, brought the matter to the attention of the public with a book entitled *The Unfortunate Experiment* (Coney, 1988) and a major inquiry followed, under Judge Sylvia Cartwright (Cartwright, 1988). The primary failing identified at the inquiry related to informed consent. Doctors in New Zealand were put on notice, unequivocally, that their long-established approaches to informed consent would no longer be accepted. The aftermath included the establishment of patient advocates and a Health and Disability Commissioner, and the ignominious end to the career of Professor Green (which had until then been illustrious). Two younger Auckland gynaecologists, although not directly implicated, subsequently gave up medicine and went to law school.

Was Professor Green very far removed from Warren, Morton, or my anaesthetic teachers? It is true that some women died of cancer who might have been saved by more conventional management; equally, some children were born who would not have been if their mothers had had hysterectomies. Outcome, however, is not the issue. The issue is that of how decisions are made in clinical practice, in clinical research and in the interface between the two.

Similar events have occurred elsewhere in the world. Of these, the inquiry into children's heart surgery at the Bristol Royal Infirmary between 1984 and 1995 is particularly well known (British Royal Infirmary Inquiry, 2001). The impact of this inquiry into medical practice in Britain has been, if anything, even greater than that of the Cartwright inquiry in New Zealand. Of fifty-three operations involving arterial switches and atrioventricular septal defects, twenty-nine resulted in the death of the patient. These results were considerably worse than those obtained in other centres. The central issue related to the persistence of these surgeons in continuing these procedures in the face of poor results, and in the information they provided to the families of prospective patients (they quoted standard risk rates rather than the rates applicable to their own institution). This was actually no more than another example of variation in practice, although it was an example in which the inquiry made it very clear (with hindsight) that the variation had gone beyond acceptable limits.

The ethical challenges faced by the Bristol cardiac surgeons and by Professor Green are not exceptional; in a general sense they are integral to surgery. By definition, the results of half of all surgeons will be below the median. Also, all surgeons go through learning curves every time they adopt a new procedure, even an established procedure. The results of a surgeon performing an operation for the thousandth time will almost certainly be better than those during his or her first ten cases. Furthermore, the best way to manage patients is not always clear-cut (and there are still those who believe Professor Green's approach to the management of low-grade abnormalities of cervical cytology was correct, if not his approach to informed consent). I expect that many parallel considerations apply to other branches of applied science.

I shall illustrate these points with one more example, related this time to surgery of the coronary arteries. Because these arteries are located on the surface of the heart it is possible to operate on them without stopping the heart from beating. Early attempts to undertake this so-called beating-heart surgery produced poor results because of the overwhelming technical challenge of grafting moving targets. The advent of the cardio-pulmonary bypass pump permitted the heart to be stopped, and coronary surgery on pump flourished, with greatly improved results. There are drawbacks to the use of bypass and the recent development of sophisticated fixation devices (such as the "Octopus") has rekindled interest in off-pump or beating-heart surgery. This now accounts for 25 to 30 per cent of all coronary surgery in the United States, yet there have been relatively few randomized trials until recently. Stated bluntly, this technique has been developed and then adopted on the basis that it seemed to be a good idea. However, in contrast to the situation faced by Warren and Morton, the benefits do not hit the observer "between the eyes". The results of such trials are now emerging, and are somewhat equivocal. There is clearly a steep learning curve for this approach to coronary surgery. Who would choose to be a surgeon's first case of off-pump surgery? Is this, then, not a situation in which widespread changes in practice should have awaited the results of randomized trials? Should surgeons be more explicit in telling patients the extent of their experience with this (or any other) technique? At an individual level, few surgeons have undertaken a rigorous audit of their rates of patient grafts with off-pump surgery (partly because the requisite angiography is expensive and carries a risk in its own right). How then are we to know if (like the Bristol surgeons) their results are falling below an acceptable limit?

The advance of surgery continues. Recently, some surgeons have begun to adopt a hybrid technique known as on-pump beating-heart surgery, for which there are only a handful of reports and no randomized studies at all. Is this a good idea? Once again, the challenge is to make progress while protecting patients from harm and surgeons from catastrophic fallout if their efforts to improve their treatments turn out to be misguided. Ethics committees clearly have a pivotal role to play, but it can be difficult to distinguish between formal experimentation (for which these committees are obviously essential), acceptable variation in day to day practice (for which they are not), and unacceptable variation in normal practice, which should simply not occur.

How are we to work this out? There are no easy answers, but perhaps we could return to mythology for assistance. I have discussed the staff of Asclepius, but there is another symbol often associated with medical practice. This symbol also involves snakes intertwined around a staff, but there are two snakes and the staff has wings. This is the caduceous of Hermes, a symbol adopted by the United States Army Medical Corp in 1902, and by a number of other medical organizations. It is fairly clear that the staff of Asclepius is the symbol better established by tradition as representing medical practice, but is it really the better of the two to represent the ethos of medicine, or to illuminate our current deliberations?

Hermes (Mercury to the Romans) was the messenger of the Olympian Gods, and was also the god of commerce, of athletes, of fertility and of thieves. The latter affiliation has led many doctors to reject his symbol as representative of medicine, often in rather wounded phraseology, but there may be lay people who would see some relevance to certain aspects of modern medicine even in this part of Hermes' portfolio! Hermes invented the lyre, brought sleep and dreams to mortals and conducted the souls of the dead to the underworld. For some reason the latter duty has also been cited by doctors as justification for rejecting his symbol, as if doctors had no role with the dying. Hermes also contributed to saving the life of the unborn Asclepius when Apollo killed his unfaithful mortal lover Coronis (Asclepius' mother). Thus, to the extent that Asclepius contributed to medicine, Hermes can also take some credit.

My own interest in Hermes, however, comes from an account related by the Canadian author, Robertson Davies, in the posthumously published book of his lectures, *The Merry Heart* (Davies, 1996). According to this account, Hermes was out walking one day, when he came across two snakes fighting. He thrust his staff between them, and they coiled themselves around it, to be held in eternal equipoise representing the struggle between two aspects of medical practice. One snake represents knowledge and, I suppose, technology and skill. The other represents wisdom. Ethical decision-making in medicine (or any other branch of applied science) depends on both. The risk we face today in health care (as in science generally) is that we may be unduly influenced by the extraordinary advances in our knowledge and technology and fail to balance the possibilities created by these with the wisdom that has informed medicine since before Hippocrates.

Thus, the staff of Asclepius has a missing snake, and I for one prefer the symbolism of the caduceous of Hermes. Lest I sound too pious, however, I would like to make one further point about Hermes. Semele was the mortal wife of Zeus. She was persuaded by Hera (another of his wives, who was jealous) to ask Zeus to reveal himself to her in all his glory. Eventually Zeus agreed, and in the event Semele was conflagrated by the brilliance of his visage. At this point Hermes rescued her unborn son (the rescuing of unborn children appears to have been a habit of his), and for this reason alone I would choose Hermes' staff over that of Asclepius as a symbol for those of us who believe that knowledge and skill in any applied science must be tempered with wisdom, and with a broadly based appreciation of life. The rescued child, you see, was none other than Dionysus, later known to the Romans as Bacchus.

## REFERENCES

Boulenger, G.A. (1913), *The Snakes of Europe*. London: Methuen & Co. Ltd. Reprinted by Arment Biological Press (2000).

Bristol Royal Infirmary Inquiry (2001), *The Report of the Public Inquiry into Children's Heart Surgery at the Bristol Royal Infirmary 1984-1995*.

Cartwright, S. (1988), *The Report of the Cervical Cancer Inquiry*. Auckland: Government Printing Office.

Coney, S. (1988), *The Unfortunate Experiment*. Auckland: Penguin.

Davies, R. (1996), *The Merry Heart*. New York: Penguin Books.

Douketis, J.D., Feightner, J.W., Attia, J. and Feldman, W.F. (1999), "Periodic Health Examination, 1999 Update: 1. Detection, Prevention and Treatment of Obesity. Appendix 1: Levels of Evidence and Grades of Recommendations of the Canadian Task Force of Preventive Health Care", *Canadian Medical Association Journal* 160:513-525.

Fenster, J.M. (2001), *Ether Day: The Strange Tale of America's Greatest Medical Discovery and the Haunted Men Who Made it*. New York: HarperCollins.

Merry, A.F. and McCall Smith, A. (2001), *Errors, Medicine and the Law*. Cambridge: Cambridge University Press.

Wilson, E.O. (1998), *Consilience*. London: Abacus.

CHAPTER 18

# Science, Ethics and Danger

L. Wolpert

Are scientists responsible for the applications of science? In a recent issue of the journal *Science*, the 1995 Nobel Peace Prize laureate, Sir Joseph Rotblat, proposes a Hippocratic oath for scientists. He is strongly opposed to the idea that science is neutral and that scientists are not to be blamed for its misapplication. Therefore he proposes an oath, or pledge, initiated by the Pugwash Group in the United States.

> I promise to work for a better world, where science and technology are used in socially responsible ways. I will not use my education for any purpose intended to harm human beings or the environment. Throughout my career, I will consider the ethical implications of my work before I take action. While the demands placed upon me might be great, I sign this declaration because I recognize that individual responsibility is the first step on the path to peace.

These are indeed noble aims to which all citizens should hope to subscribe, but the oath does present some severe difficulties in relation to science. Rotblat does not want to distinguish between scientific knowledge and its application, technology. He ignores the fact that the very nature of science is that it is not possible to predict what will be discovered or how these discoveries could be applied. Cloning provides a nice example. The original studies related to cloning were largely the work of biologists in the 1960s. They were studying how frog embryos develop and wanted to find out if genes which are located in the cell nucleus were lost or permanently turned off as the embryo developed. It was incidental to the experiment that the frog that developed was a clone of the animal from which the nucleus was obtained. The history of science is filled with such examples.

The poet, Paul Valery's remark that "We enter the future backwards" is very apposite in relation to the possible applications of science. Scientists cannot easily predict the social and technological implications of their current research. It was originally argued that radio waves would have no practical applications and Lord Rutherford said that applications of atomic energy were moonshine. There was, again, no way that those investigating the ability of certain bacteria to resist infection by viruses would lead to the discovery of the restriction enzymes, an indispensable tool for cutting up DNA, the genetic material fundamental to genetic engineering.

Part of the problem is the all too common conflation of science and technology (Wolpert, 1992). The distinction between science and technology, between knowledge and understanding on the one hand, and the application of that knowledge to making something, or using it in some practical way, is fundamental. Science produces ideas about how the world works, whereas the ideas in technology result in usable objects. Technology is much older than anything one could regard as science; and unaided by any science, technology gave rise to the crafts of early humans such as agriculture and metalworking. Science made little contribution to technology until the nineteenth century. And even the great triumphs of engineering, like the steam engine and Renaissance cathedrals, were built without impact from science. It was imaginative trial and error. It is technology that carries with it ethical issues, from motor cars to cloning a human.

By contrast, reliable scientific knowledge is value-free and has no moral or ethical value. Science tells us how the world is. That we are not at the centre of the universe is neither good nor bad, nor is the possibility that genes can influence our intelligence or our behaviour. Dangers and ethical issues only arise when science is applied as technology. However, ethical issues can arise in actually doing the scientific research, such as doing experiments on humans or animals, as well as issues related to safety. In this respect scientists have very similar ethical problems to those of all citizens.

The social and ethical obligations that scientists have as distinct from those responsibilities they share with all citizens, such as supporting a democratic society and taking due care of the rights of others, comes from them having access to specialized knowledge of how the world works that is not easily accessible to others. Their obligation is to both make public any social implications of their work and its technological applications and to give some assessment of its reliability. In most areas of science it matters little to the public whether a particular theory is right or wrong but in some areas such as human and plant genetics, it matters a great deal. Whatever new technology is introduced, it is not for the scientists to make the moral or ethical decisions. They have neither special rights nor skills in areas involving moral or ethical issues. There is, in fact, a grave danger in asking scientists to be more socially responsible if that means that they have the right and power to take such decisions on their own. Moreover, scientists rarely have power in relation to the applications of science; this rests with those with the money: industry and government. The way scientific knowledge is used raises ethical issues for everyone involved, not just scientists.

It is not easy to find examples of scientists as a group behaving immorally or in a dangerous manner, but there is the eugenics movement. The scientific assumptions behind this proposal are crucial; the assumption is that most desirable and undesirable human attributes are inherited. Not only was talent perceived of as being inherited but so too were pauperism, insanity and any kind of so-called feeble-mindedness. They completely failed to give an assessment of the reliability of their ideas. To the contrary, and even more blameworthy, their conclusions seem to have been driven by what they saw as the desirable social implications. By contrast, in relation to the building of the atomic bomb, the allied scientists behaved morally and fulfilled their social obligations by informing their governments about the implications of atomic theory. The decision to build the bomb was taken by politicians, not scientists, and it was an enormous engineering enterprise. Had they decided not to participate in constructing an atomic weapon would the war have been lost? Should scientists on their own ever be entitled to make such decisions?

Genetics seems to raise many ethical issues. Mary Shelley would be both proud and shocked. Her creation of a scientist, Frankenstein, creating and meddling with human life has become the most potent symbol of modern science. Her brilliant fantasy has become so distorted that even those who are normally quite sensible lose all sense when the idea of cloning humans appears before them. The image of Frankenstein has been turned by the media into genetic pornography whose real aim is to titillate, excite and frighten.

Ironically, the real clone of sheep has been the media who blindly and unthinkingly follow each other; how embarrassed Dolly ought to be. The moral masturbators have been out in force telling us of the horrors of cloning (Wolpert, 2000). Some in the United States demanded a worldwide ban and suggested that cloning should carry a penalty on a par with rape, child abuse and murder. Many others, national leaders included, have joined in that chorus of horror. But what horrors? What ethical issues? In all the righteous indignation I have not found a single new, relevant ethical issue spelled out.

In the case of humans, the really important issue is how the child will be cared for. Given the terrible things that humans are reported to do to each other, cloning should take a very low priority in our list of anxieties. Or perhaps it is a way of displacing our real problems with unreal ones. Having a child raises real ethical problems as it is the parents who play God, not the scientists. Here lies a bitter irony. A parent's relation to a child is infinitely more God-like than anything that scientists may discover. Parents hold tremendous power over young children. They do not always exercise it to the child's benefit.

This aspect of parental care is very relevant to the so-called ethical issues raised by designer babies. I cannot see why a parent should not be able to choose a child to have genes that promote good health and avoid those that lead to disease. And why should they not seek intelligence or blue eyes, although the former, involving thousands of genes, is most impractical. Much more serious and neglected is the right of couples, who are child abusers or drug addicts and with serious genetic illnesses, to have children. There are tens of thousands of children referred to social services each year and about 10 per cent of all children suffer from some sort of abuse: physical, emotional, psychological. These are the real issues in relation to reproduction.

Cloning of a human raises no new ethical issues, but should be opposed on the ground of the risk of the child developing abnormally. The use of stem cells and therapeutic cloning to make stem cells that could provide tissues to replace damaged organs without the increased risk of immune rejection raises no such problems. No politician has publicly pointed out or even understood that the so-called ethical issues involved in therapeutic cloning are indistinguishable from those that are involved in *in vitro* fertilization (IVF) as both involve desecration of embryos. One could even argue that IVF is less ethical than therapeutic cloning. But no reasonable person could possibly want to ban IVF when it has helped so many infertile couples. Where are the politicians who will stand up and say this?

And what are the objections to making embryonic stem cells? The fertilized egg is not a human being. Would one not rather accept a thousand abortions and the destruction of all unwanted frozen embryos than a single unwanted child who will be neglected or abused? I take the same view in regard to severely crippling and painful genetic diseases. On what ground should parents be allowed to have a severely disabled child when it could be relatively easily prevented by prenatal diagnosis? It is nothing to do with consumerism but the interests and rights of the child.

What dangers does genetics pose? Bioethics is a growth industry but one should regard the field with caution as the bioethicists have a vested interest in finding difficulties. Anxieties about designer babies are at present premature as it is far too risky, and it may be necessary, in the first instance, to accept what has been called procreative autonomy, a couple's right to control their own role in procreation unless the state has a compelling reason for denying them that control. Gene therapy, introducing genes to cure a genetic disease like cystic fibrosis, carries risks as do all new medical treatments. There may well be problems with insurance and testing, but are these any different from those related to someone suspected of having AIDS? One must wonder why the bio-moralists do not devote their attention to other technical advances like that convenient form of transport which claims over fifty thousand killed or seriously injured each year. Could it be that in this case they themselves would be inconvenienced?

There are surveys that show some distrust of scientists, particularly those in government and industry. This probably relates to bovine spongiform encephalopathy and genetically modified foods and therefore, one must ask how this affects an individual's behaviour. I need to be persuaded that many of those who have this claimed distrust would refuse, if ill, to take a drug that had been made from a genetically modified plant or would reject a tomato so modified that it was cheap and would help prevent heart disease. Who refuses insulin or growth hormone because it is made of genetically modified bacteria? It is easy to be negative about science if it does not affect one's actions.

Genetically modified foods have raised extensive public concerns and there seems no alternative but to rely on regulatory bodies to assess their safety as happens with other food products. Similar considerations apply to the release of genetically modified organisms. Genetic engineering requires considerable scientific and technical knowledge and, even more important, money that scientists in general do not have. Indeed, for the public sector, the applications of genetics and molecular biology can open up difficult choices because such applications are expensive. New medical treatments, requiring complex technology, cannot be given to all. There has to be some principle of rationing and this really does pose serious moral and ethical dilemmas much more worthy of consideration than the dangers posed by genetic engineering.

Are there areas of research that are so socially sensitive that research into them should be avoided, even proscribed? One possible area is that of the genetic basis of intelligence and particularly the possible link between race and intelligence. Are there then, as the literary critic George Steiner has argued, "certain orders of truth which would infect the marrow of politics and would poison beyond all cure the already tense relations between social classes and these communities"? In short are there doors immediately in front of current research which should be marked "Too dangerous to open"? I realize the dangers, but I cherish the openness of scientific investigation too much to put up such a notice. I stand by the distinction between knowledge of the world and how it is used. Therefore I must say "No" to Steiner's question, provided of course that scientists fulfil their social obligations. The main reason is that the better understanding there is of the world, the better chance there is of making a just society, the better chance of improved living conditions. One should not abandon the possibility of doing good by applying some scientific idea because it can also be used to do wrong. All techniques can be abused and there is no knowledge or information that is not susceptible to manipulation for evil purposes. I can do terrible damage to someone by using my glasses as a weapon. Once one begins to censor the acquisition of reliable scientific knowledge, one is on the most slippery of slippery slopes.

To those who doubt whether the public or politicians are capable of taking the correct decisions in relation to science and its applications I strongly commend Thomas Jefferson's advice. "There is no known safe depository of the ultimate powers of society but the people themselves, and if we think them not enlightened enough to exercise that control with a wholesome discretion, the remedy is not to take it from them, but to inform their direction." But how does one ensure that the public is involved in decision-making? How can one ensure that scientists, doctors, engineers, bioethicists and other experts, who must be involved, do not appropriate decision-making for themselves? How do we ensure that scientists take on the social obligation of making the implications of their work public? One has to rely on the many institutions of a democratic society: parliament, a free and vigorous press, affected groups and the scientists themselves.

## REFERENCES

Wolpert, L. (1992), *The Unnatural Nature of Science*. London: Faber.
_____ (2002), "Is Science Dangerous?" *Journal of Molecular Biology* 319:969-972.

# PART VII

## NATURAL DISASTERS, TERRORISM AND PUBLIC SAFETY

CHAPTER 19

# Operational Research Approaches to Complex and Uncertain Problems

B. Farbey

## INTRODUCTION

One curious and unexpected effect of growing older is finding one's earlier years becoming part of "history".[1] Operational Research (OR), the discipline into which I was recruited as a newly-minted statistician in 1959, and which was then in its heyday, now has a history stretching back more than sixty years.[2] Experimental techniques which were at the leading edge of scientific application when I joined the profession, for example, computer-based simulation, are now widely accepted almost commonplace and frequently mechanical.

This paper looks back to the original OR approach as a multi-disciplinary, scientific exercise in modelling and then to more recent developments in order to find a way to analyze contemporary problems of natural disasters, terrorism and public safety. The paper briefly traces the origins of OR, starting just before the Second World War, and lists the techniques that have become central. It observes that the modern discipline comprises both "hard" and "soft" Operational Research and that each has a role to play depending on the degree of uncertainty as to outcome, cause and effect.

## ORIGINS

Histories of Operational Research generally place its beginnings in military research in the late 1930s (Cummings, 2001; Trefethen, 1954; Beer, 1967). Cummings states that the "term Operational Research would appear to have been coined for the first time in 1938, as a descriptive term for the use of scientists to assess, at first hand, military situations and the deployment of devices therein" (Cummings, 2001).

These early studies established many of the defining characteristics of the new discipline. Studies on radar detection, for example, dealt with incomplete information and took an experimental approach. Research into convoy losses and optimal plane formations led to an appreciation of the importance of modelling. Studies of gunnery found discrepancies between the way equipment performed in the laboratory and then operationally in the field. Crucially, these early days established a pattern of interdisciplinary working, which was unusual then, and even now is hard to recreate as narrower and narrower specializations abound. Trefethen (1954) tells the story of "Blackett's circus", the team assembled by P.M.S. Blackett, which included three physiologists, one astrophysicist, one Army officer, one surveyor, one general physicist and two mathematicians, an assembly only equalled perhaps by the annual gatherings at Herstmonceux Castle!

The war over, Operational Research moved rapidly into government and industry, being particularly successful in the British steel and coal industries (Cummings, 2001). Civilian use of OR gradually moved to provide the foundations of a management science, and added a further ingredient: the attention to strategy and to cybernetics, both of which ordained a holistic approach to problems (Beer, 1967).

## HARD OPERATIONAL RESEARCH

Early textbooks clearly saw Operational Research as a science (e.g., Sasieni, Yaspan and Friedman, 1959; or Wilson, 1973). Sasieni *et al.* write that "most practical operations research consists of identifying the decision-makers, discovering their (possibly conflicting) objectives, and translating these objectives into points along compatible scales" (Sasieni *et al.*, 1959, p. 2), and recommend "that some acquaintance with the main concepts and results of the calculus" (ibid., p. 3).

Wilson, writing more than ten years later, says that "[OR is] really a science based on mathematical truisms that has amalgamated a range of known and new techniques into a quantitative management tool box"(Wilson, 1973, p. 1). He goes on to say firmly that "the true O.R. man has to be, basically, a mathematician. However, O.R. work is best done by a team which should include staff drawn from a number of disciplines — for example a statistician, a works study specialist, a production engineer, and an accountant" (ibid., p. 1). Wilson lists the techniques as: (i) mathematical statistics, (ii) applied statistics, (iii) reliability theory, (iv) inventory control theory, (v) replacement theory, (vi) queuing theory, (vii) critical path scheduling theory, and (viii) mathematical programming, including linear, non-linear, discrete and stochastic programming, as well as dynamic programming (ibid., p. 2).

I would then add to his list: (i) the theory of games and decisions, (ii) simulation and (iii) systems dynamics. Applications of hard OR can easily be found in the study of natural disasters, terrorism and public safety. Mathematical programming, games and decision theory are used to study disaster recovery planning. Games and decision theory are used in military planning, and simulation and geographical information systems are used in planning for real-time disasters.

## SOFT OPERATIONAL RESEARCH

Despite its successes, particularly during the "golden age" of the 1960s and 1970s (Rosenhead, 1989), hard OR gradually slipped from the public view. It was at the same time much criticized for its concentration on techniques and a lack of appreciation by academics of the practical difficulties associated with an essentially practical endeavour. The decline was matched by a split amongst practitioners. Rosenhead presents a powerful argument against the ever-narrowing focus on technique, seeing OR as "shackled to its tool-box of models/techniques/solutions" (Rosenhead, 1989, p. 6). In stressing the significance of context in the formulation of problems, he quotes Ackoff's "characterization of OR as 'mathematically sophisticated but contextually naive'" (ibid., p. 5).

In *Rational Analysis for a Problematic World*, Rosenhead has gathered a set of alternative, "soft" OR techniques, all of which do take account of context and do not necessarily view the approach or procedures as scientific. He claims that the hard OR concept of the "well-structured problem" is simply unavailable in the complexity of real-life organizations and looks to an alternative paradigm of careful problem structuring, more suited to problems that are in Ackoff's term "messes", that is to say "complex systems of changing problems that interact with each other" (Ackoff, as quoted in Rosenhead 1989, p. 10).

The collection of soft OR approaches found in Rosenhead (1989) comprises:

- cognitive mapping, a method for mapping an individual or group's perception of a problem, essentially as a graph with nodes and arcs;
- soft systems methodology, a procedure for learning about a complex situation with a view to eventual purposeful action;
- strategic choice, which deals with the interconnectedness of strategic problems;
- robustness analysis, a methodology for "keeping your options open" and not becoming so committed to a particular course of action that you cannot backtrack should circumstances change; and
- metagames which incorporate scenarios into the exploration of conflicting positions in order to find a mode of co-operation.

I would add the earlier stages of systems dynamics modelling which I have seen performed using a "soft algebra", that is to say, using drawings and symbols with groups of executives to establish the model and a common mental picture of the phenomenon under study.

Soft OR has been used in situations where there is potential conflict, for example, in policing of public events, in industrial consulting (Checkland, 1989) and in the development of information systems (Davies and Ledington, 1991).

## SELECTING AN APPROPRIATE APPROACH

Given the two variants of Operational Research and the kinds of problems that arise in the case of disasters, natural or man-made, how might one choose between them? Rosenhead reminds us of an analysis by Hopwood (1980).[3] A later version of the same theme occurs in Earl and Hopwood (1987) which is partially reproduced below in Table 1. The table indicates the type of situation that one might face, and the type of decision available. Thus, where the objectives of an action are reasonably clear, and where the effect is also calculable, a decision by computation using traditional, hard OR methods is a sensible way to proceed. One could speculate, for example, that once a need for aid is determined following a disaster, OR techniques would work well in planning and optimizing the relief effort.

Table 1: Decision Types

| | | Uncertainty as to Cause and Effect | |
| | | *Low* | *High* |
| --- | --- | --- | --- |
| | *Low* | decision by computation | decision by judgement |
| *Uncertainty as to Objectives* | | | |
| | *High* | decision by compromise | decision by inspiration |

Note: This is a partial reproduction from Earl and Hopwood (1987).

However, where there is uncertainty as to the objectives or ambiguity of goals ("ambiguity" is Hellstern's term), there needs to be dialogue and consensus before proceeding to a mechanical solution (Hellstern, 1986). Speculating again, a natural disaster or act of terror would likely involve many different people and interests, including victims, relatives, local, national and regional governments, and international bodies. These situations might well be better tackled first with a softer approach, in order to reach a well-understood working agreement from which everyone could proceed. Public safety issues such as ensuring safety at a large sporting event, would also benefit from a soft approach in the early planning stages.

High uncertainty as to cause and effect requires judgement (Earl and Hopwood, 1987), plus if possible, experimental evaluation (Hellstern, 1986). New sporting venues, for example, are sometimes tested with volunteer "crowds", before they are opened to the general public.

Finally, where there is uncertainty as to cause and effect, and where the objectives are themselves not clear, one would attempt to set procedures in motion that would reduce the uncertainty, or clarify the goals, but in the end inspiration may be the only way forward.

In summary, hard Operational Research techniques are most useful when problems are well structured and amenable to quantitative modelling. Soft approaches seem to be more suited to problems for which statistical modelling of causality is not likely to prove feasible, or problems that have a low probability of occurrence and are of high consequence when they do occur.

## NOTES

1. It may be that history itself is speeding up. Some years ago a colleague and I interviewed the senior manager of the history department of a large news agency. "How long", asked my colleague, "is history?" Our friend did not hesitate, "six minutes".
2. Operational Research is the British usage. In North America and elsewhere it is more often referred to as Operations Research
3. A very similar analysis, but in the different context of evaluation theory, occurs in Hellstern (1986).

## REFERENCES

Ackoff, R. (1979), "The Future of Operational Research is Past", *Journal of the Operational Research Society* 30(2):93-104.

Beer, S. (1967), *Management Science: The Business Use of Operations Research*. London: Aldus Books.

Checkland, P. (1989), "Soft Systems Methodology", in *Rational Analysis for a Problematic World*, ed. J. Rosenhead. Chichester, UK: John Wiley & Sons.

Cummings, N. (2001), "How the World of OR Societies Began", in *OR Newsletter*, April, 1997. Available at <*http://www.orsoc.org.uk/about/topic/news/orclub/htm*> accessed 22.10.2003.

Davies L. and Ledington, P. (1991), *Information in Action: Soft Systems Methodology*. Houndmills, Basingstoke: Macmillan Education Ltd.

Earl, M. and Hopwood, A. (1987), "From Management Information to Information Management", in *Towards Strategic Information Systems*, ed. E.K. Somogyi and R.D. Galliers. Tunbridge Wells, UK and Cambridge, MA: Abacus Press.

Hellstern, G.-M. (1986), "Assessing Evaluation Research", in *Guidance, Control and Evaluation in the Public Sector*, ed. F.X. Kaufmann, G. Majone and V. Ostrom. New York: de Gruyter, pp. 279-312.

Hopwood, A.G. (1980), "The Organisational and Behavioural Aspects of Budgeting and Control", in *Topics in Management Accounting*, ed. J. Arnold, B. Carsberg and R. Scapens. Deddington, UK: Philip Allen, pp. 221-240.

Rosenhead, J. (1989), "Introduction: Old and New Paradigms for Analysis", in *Rational Analysis for a Problematic World*, ed. J. Rosenhead. Chichester, UK: John Wiley & Sons.

Sasieni, M., Yaspan, A. and Friedman, L. (1959), *Operations Research: Methods and Problems*. New York: John Wiley & Sons, Inc.

Trefethen, F. N. (1954), "A History of Operations Research", in *Operations Research for Management*, ed. J.F. McCloskey and F.N. Trefethen. Baltimore, MD: Johns Hopkins Press.

Wilson, C. (1973), *Operational Research for Students of Management*. Aylesbury, UK: Intertext Books.

CHAPTER 20

# The Challenges of Addressing Terrorism, Natural Disasters and Public Safety through Public Policy

R.T. Haworth

## NATURAL DISASTERS AND SCIENCE

A sad fact of contemporary life is that reported natural disasters are often, in the first instance, believed to be acts of terrorism. The loss of the aircraft Swiss Air 111 off Nova Scotia on September 2, 1998, was not a repeat of the "Air India" situation, but was quickly discerned to have been a disaster caused by a technical failure. The crew of Swiss Air 111 reported smoke in the cockpit and attempted to make an emergency landing at Halifax International Airport. The track of the aircraft and the conversations between the crew and the local traffic controllers are a matter of public record, but verbal contact with the aircraft was terminated well before the end of the flight and the aircraft was lost from the radar screen. Swiss Air 111 was essentially lost. Subsequently, it was confirmed that the aircraft had come down in St. Margarets Bay, Nova Scotia.

Technology, based on significant scientific endeavour, played an enormous role in unravelling the events of the day. For example, without any voice or radar contact, the most precise timing of the crash was provided by the national earthquake monitoring network. Using last minute information on the route of the aircraft and the approximate time of the crash (from sightings by local residents) the precise time and location of the impact, together with additional evidence that related to the nature of the impact were obtained. That laid the groundwork for the second contribution of science and technology. Canadian scientists had developed a method by which a wide (swath) image of the sea floor could be obtained. This "swath-mapping" system, the envy of the world at the time, was used to map the entire sea-floor of the bay and indicate areas where debris might be found. The aircraft fuselage was recovered over a four-year period and reassembled in a hangar at the Shearwater Forces base in Dartmouth, Nova Scotia. In this case, two scientific developments were applied in unforeseen situations to provide critical information about a natural disaster.

Early in my research career, I was impressed by an article entitled "The Importance of Being Aimless" which noted that many scientific breakthroughs are spawned when there is no specific objective. The breakthroughs themselves are, however, applicable to many diverse objectives. That perspective is often emphasized by experiences such as this, but it also underlines the responsibility of scientists to be "translators" for their profession. They also need to be aware of and promote the social application of their work.

## TERRORISM, PUBLIC POLICY AND STATISTICS

In 1998, the international diamond industry produced an estimated one hundred and fifteen million carats of rough diamonds with a market value of U.S.$6.7 billion which when converted to jewelry were worth close to U.S.$50 billion. In 1990, scientists in Canada were still searching beneath the glacial rubble of northern Canada for the first diamonds that we knew must be there: all other areas of the world with a similar geology had found them, why not us? In 1991, the search was successful and in 1998 Canada's first operating diamond mine, Ekati, opened in the Northwest Territories, 300 kilometres northeast of Yellowknife. Ekati employs six hundred and fifty people and produces over three million carats of gem-quality rough diamonds each year valued at U.S.$500 million, representing nearly 4 per cent of world production by weight and 6 per cent by value. A second mine, Diavik, began operation in early 2003. Two more could open by 2007 by which time it is anticipated that they will probably provide direct employment for about sixteen hundred people and bring total annual production to approximately U.S.$1 billion, making Canada the third highest diamond producer in the world. Canada exports its entire production of diamonds for sorting before some gem-quality diamonds are returned to Canada in support of a small but growing cutting and polishing industry. Any interruption in trade of diamonds would therefore have dire implications for a Canadian diamond industry that supports significant Aboriginal employment.

Such a threat was posed by the impact of trade in "conflict" diamonds, those rough diamonds used by rebel movements to finance conflicts aimed at undermining government activities. This illicit trade has had a devastating impact on peace and human security in several African nations, including Angola, Sierra Leone and the Democratic Republic of Congo (DRC). Diamonds from eastern Sierra Leone, smuggled into Liberia by mainly Lebanese traders, funded the activities of the Revolutionary United Front in Sierra Leone. By the early 1990s, Liberia had become a major centre for massive diamond-related criminal activity, with connections to guns, drugs and money laundering, fuelling war and providing a safe haven for organized crime. A similar situation existed in Angola, a country with extraordinary potential resource wealth, in which 10 per cent of the population was killed by a war fuelled by the proceeds of resource development. World reaction against this aspect of the diamond market threatened to undermine the social and economic benefits derived from the other 95 per cent of the diamond market, including that of Canada.

Canada played a leadership role in international efforts to curb this illicit trade, even before diamonds were mined in Canada. The Kimberley Process, led by South Africa, and supported by forty-eight countries, including Canada, representing 98 per cent of the world's diamond trade market, was designed to isolate and hence prohibit this trade. It is designed to ensure that only diamonds certified by governments as having originated in legitimate operations would be allowed to enter the diamond-trading world. Participating countries are required to export rough diamonds in tamper-resistant containers and provide a certificate, validated by the government of the exporting country, confirming that the diamond exports are conflict-free. Participating countries were to prohibit import of rough diamonds from countries not engaged in the Kimberley Process by the end of 2002.

Introduction of domestic legislation to implement the Kimberley Process in Canada was the epitome of interdepartmental co-operation in policy-making. Every step of the legislative process could not have been completed between June 2002 and December 31, 2002 if an "impossible" schedule had not been met. This was made even more difficult since ratification of the Kyoto Protocol was making its way through

Parliament during the same period. Despite all the challenges, Bill C-14 — an act providing for controls on the export, import or transit across Canada of rough diamonds and for a certification scheme for the export of rough diamonds in order to meet Canada's obligations under the Kimberley Process — was introduced into the House of Commons on October 10, 2003 and received Royal Assent on December 13, 2002. Related regulations came into effect on January 1, 2003. A significant challenge in the implementation procedure has been to establish a statistical process to track the movement of diamonds. Canada's leadership in addressing the chaotic effects of mis-classification of diamonds as minerals, and the sophistication of our mineral databases, has resulted in our being asked to oversee this process internationally.

Yet, despite fifty governments having stated in November 2002 that they would be ready by January 1, 2003, only Canada, India, Australia, Switzerland and a few countries in Africa began implementing the provisions on that date. Partnership Canada Africa commented that:

> Being closer to the issue of conflict diamonds and to the wars in Angola and the DRC, Botswana knows the havoc that an unregulated diamond trade can wreak. Perhaps conversely, countries like the [United States] that were not ready on January 1, or even February 1, simply don't take other people's wars and fights against terrorism seriously.

## PUBLIC SAFETY AND PUBLIC POLICY

Natural Resources Canada administers the federal *Explosives Act* and regulations, primarily because of the use of explosives in mining. The act regulates the importation, manufacture, storage, movement and sale of explosives, principally aimed at health and safety. Explosives include blasting explosives, propellants, ammunition, fireworks and pyrotechnics. In the aftermath of the events of September 11, 2001, it became evident that the *Explosives Act* required amendments to boost security provisions necessary to better protect the domestic explosives supply from criminal and terrorist interests. These amendments would help bring Canada into compliance with the Inter-America Convention Against the Illicit Manufacturing of and Trafficking in Firearms, Ammunition, Explosives and Other Related Materials which it signed as part of the Organization of American States in 1997.

At present, most Canadians may purchase and possess explosives without any background security check. In Quebec, since the FLQ crisis, individuals wishing to handle explosives may only be issued with an explosives permit after an appropriate security check. This system has operated without incident for thirty years. The proposed federal amendments introduce this and other controls over the acquisition and possession of explosives and their components.

However, development and introduction of the amendments highlighted unexpected stakeholders in the process. The principal constituent of most commercial explosives is ammonium nitrate. This is commonly used as a fertilizer, but was the principal component of the explosives that killed one hundred and sixty-eight people in Oklahoma City in April 1995. Most ammonium nitrate is supplied to farms in bulk; less than 1 per cent is retail sale, typically in 25 kilogram bags. The challenge was to control the latter without compromising the 99 per cent agricultural market. The solution was to engage the Canadian Food Inspection Agency in getting vendors to keep sales records and to request proof of identity from those purchasing bagged fertilizer who are unknown to the vendor.

Recent tightening of border security with the United States caused a few problems. From the outset, we had sought to ensure compatibility between U.S. and Canadian regulations. However, when responsibility for that regulation was transferred to the new Department of Homeland Security, they denied access to the United States of all aliens in possession of explosives. This included the truck drivers transhipping explosives to the United States from Canadian ports. Canadian eastern ports have deeper waters and are more remote than those in the eastern United States. Consequently, explosive cargos were denied access to the United States in January 2003, a time when the U.S. military was embarking upon a major military expedition! When proposing regulations, one has to be aware of the breadth of use of explosives. Some, such as in fireworks, are relatively obvious. Other explosives used by the oil and gas industry to perforate the casings of wells may be less well known. In the mineral exploration industry, small quantities of explosives are used for everything from geophysical exploration to removing trees. In the automotive industry, a small explosive charge is used to inflate an airbag! However, even the trap and skeet shooters were affected, because of potential interference with their ability to refill their own cartridges.

EPILOGUE

In developing public policy with respect to terrorism and public safety, or in applying science and technology to natural disasters, these few examples show that one must always be prepared for the unexpected. Some things work "for better" and some things work "for worse". But in most of the policy development in which I have participated, science has played a significant role in either the development or implementation of these policies. For example, much can and is being done about the detection and fingerprinting of explosives. In contrast, trying to fingerprint the locality at which a diamond originated has been challenging and unsuccessful to date.

Much of the policy-making I deal with daily has sustainable development at its heart, that is, development that satisfies the needs of the present without compromising the ability of future generations to meet their needs. I hope that this is a principle that will eventually become universally practised. Yet, turning what is surely an acceptable and righteous principle into practice is a major challenge. Often this is because those implicated fail to recognize the part that they play, and that the critical choices often lie in their hands. However, when they do, they often do a better job voluntarily than when responding to regulations that implement laws. If this trend can continue, rather than "for better or for worse" the phrase "patient heal thyself" may become the catch-phrase for policy development.

CHAPTER 21

# The Front Line in the War on Bioterrorism

R.J. Howard

In the United States, there are over eighty agencies or entities of the federal government involved in the war on terrorism. There is perhaps a no more frightening scenario to the American public than that of a possible intentional contamination of food, water, air or environment. Terrorist agents, both foreign and domestic, have at their disposal a wide range of viral, bacterial and parasitic agents which when used with the intent to harm, could do so on a massive scale. To a great extent, the American public believes that detection of such an event will be recognized by a federal agent, member of the military or intelligence agency. Virtually every expert in government has recognized that this simply will not be the case, detection will more likely occur in the office of a practising physician or in an emergency room of a hospital. When questioned by members of the public at virtually every public event, President George W. Bush, Homeland Security Director Tom Ridge and incoming President of the American Medical Association, Dr. Don Palmasano have stressed the role of the community physician and the need to keep them alert to the sounds of both "horses and zebras".

It is vital therefore that physicians at all levels take seriously the call to be vigilant and alert for these threats. At the core of medical education on the issue of bioterrorism lie ten overriding factors that will direct us toward a programme of success and improved service to patients, communities and the nation. These themes must begin in medical school and have application and practice throughout the training of physicians and be made a part of comprehensive medical continuing education. These core themes are:

*Basic Medical Education.* It is important to think through the existing medical school curricula and ensure that enough attention is being paid to both the pathogens and the ability of the doctors who are being sent into hospitals and clinics to recognize and treat them. Doctors must be empowered by continuing education to recognize any new and/or emerging threat which may be used by a rogue nation, group or individual to do harm.

*Surveillance.* Physicians at all levels must understand that there exists within the United States of America a responsive public health system which can be used in any health crisis, but is of little use if a doctor is unaware of how to notify, alert and use these resources. Recent efforts on the part of the federal government have placed many strategic supplies at widely distributed, but quickly accessible, locations for this very purpose. Rapid response and surveillance is at the core of every public health success and each physician must know what is available at the local, state and national levels.

*Detection.* Effective detection means that each physician has the clinical and laboratory skills accessible in order that they may evaluate a potential threat. Local and state laboratories have to rely on the federal agencies to provide findings when testing efforts can be achieved locally. Better use of computer technology like PULSENET should be made which can electronically compare findings during a food-borne outbreak across samples taken in many states.

*Recognition.* Physicians must be trained to observe carefully and recognize the frequently subtle signs that separate the broad spectrum of similar diseases. For example: What separates a common cold from a hanta virus infection; or an influenza virus from an anthrax bacterium? Medical societies, groups and physicians must be quick to provide training and not criticize staff or be punitive in comments or action when legitimate questions are raised. Once again, rapid diagnostic kits or tools can be stockpiled and made available to doctors on short notice.

*Diagnosis and Characterization.* Textbooks, manuals and publications within the clinic and hospital environment must be developed to assist the physician and staff in rapid diagnosis and characterization of a potential biological agent. Textbooks, manuals and on-site documents which are quickly accessed and user friendly, will be necessary for a physician to rapidly assess the nature of a pathogen and when combined with rapid laboratory diagnostic tools will prove to be an invaluable life-saving tool. Linking all of these systems within a city, county, state and hospital will be the ultimate goal of a programme that uses all of the technology and resources a physician will need to move forward with a correct and appropriate diagnosis and characterization of a presented illness.

*Reporting*. Physicians must be keenly aware of the "need for speed" in reporting suspected bioterrorism events. When public health at local, state and federal levels are alerted quickly and efficiently, there will be time to triage, discuss and evaluate the appropriate actions which the variety of government roles will need to play in each potential outbreak. There must be a concerted effort to engender an environment where physicians and staff feel free to share concerns and report suspicious findings in a timely and effective fashion. Methods of reporting need to be taught, encouraged and praised when done correctly. The more time public health units, working with local partners, have to react and respond to an outbreak the greater will be the number of lives saved.

*Treatment*. Resources and protocols for treatment, stabilization and even transportation or relocation of suspected patients within a hospital or clinic will prove to be vital in containing an outbreak. Physicians and administrations, along with infection-control personnel, must know how to treat, react and respond during an outbreak and understand what real threats each outbreak might pose to the staff. These efforts must be discussed, practised and evaluated in order to make them efficient and timely. It is especially important to realize that in an outbreak situation, supplies of treatments and antibiotics, anti-virals and other medicines will invariably come into short supply and staff will have to rely on outside and previously discussed and explored venues of supply and delivery.

*Response*. Each institution should evaluate how to respond best within the community. Each hospital needs to know what local, community and internal resources they have available to them and how quickly they can put these resources to use. An honest and comprehensive evaluation of what the institution can do and what is needed is critical before effective plans can be made. Each doctor and administrator should assess resources and skills and ask "What will be needed in the event of ...?" and then take appropriate action to ensure that any gap is filled or question answered. The public will have zero tolerance for an institution that has not asked these questions in the post-9/11 world.

*Communication.* At no other time except during a real or suspected biological attack will a clinic or hospital communication staff be more tested and stressed. Every possible rumour will arise and every media outlet will descend to explore, exploit and report these rumours. It is critical that clear lines of communication be established between medical staff and the administration and between the administration and the public through the news media. There must be a solid and well-practised system of institutional community integrity where all hospital staff understand how and where information flows and how it will be communicated to the public. It is vital to set-up, practise and evaluate what actions the media will take in a crisis situation and how the institution can best provide clear and concise information and counsel to the public at the time when it is most needed. It is also important to understand that the institution must be able to meet the immediate demands of the media and to move at their speed. The media abhor a vacuum and tend to fill it with misinformation. Eliminate the need for speculation with clear and precise information.

*Evaluation.* Every institution should take the important step of evaluating exercises and asking the hard questions when problems arise. Each evaluation should be done with multiple sets of eyes and skill sets. No complete bioterrorism exercise can be done without thorough involvement of the laboratory along with the emergency room and administrative and public relations offices.

Ultimately, each physician and every institution will have to ask the question "How prepared am I?" The answer to this question is more effective if the advice of those who have undergone real world emergency situations is taken. Those who have been tested in these situations have insight and advice that is timely and essential. By adhering to the principles of thoughtful education, ongoing awareness and the efficient application of solid medical and diagnostic skills, medical personnel will be able to serve both their patients and their communities in a compassionate and effective way.

# PART VIII

## CRIME AND MORALITY

CHAPTER 22

# Is Duty Dead?

V.M. Del Buono

## INTRODUCTION

What do law, ethics, science, statistics and public policy all have in common? They each involve the application of reason to human experience. This distinguishes science from religion and magic, ethics from morality and the rule of law from the exercise of arbitrary power. The grounding in human experience distinguishes statistics from mathematics, science from metaphysics and law from logic. Furthermore, as I see it, the entire purpose of public policy is to seek to influence some aspect of human behaviour in order to achieve a public good.

The combinations and permutations of subjects that one could talk about given a topic like crime and morality are huge. For example, I have spent considerable time thinking about all of the assumptions about human behaviour, the exigencies of public policy and evidentiary and procedural rules for fixing personal responsibility for behaviour in order that it be found to be criminal. I also believe that the policy and practical issues surrounding the delivery of policing and other justice sector services are among some of the most difficult in the public policy sphere. If the title of the conference had been simply "law and public policy", then either of the topics might have been completely appropriate. But the title also includes the word "ethics"; therefore, I will explore the question: "Is the concept of 'duty' and all that it implies for ethics, law and science, dead?"

The question is not an idle one for I would argue that the word "duty" has almost entirely disappeared from everyday speech. The only vestige is the rather prosaic duties as found in job descriptions. In the professional speech of law, the only common occurrence is the phrase "duty of care" which is at the heart of the law of negligence, but even that is hardly the stuff of every day discourse.

Contrast the near disappearance of duty from our everyday speech, with the spectacular growth since the adoption of the Universal Declaration of Human Rights fifty-five years ago of the use of the word "right" or more commonly, as it occurs in its plural "rights". All of us have rights, many of which are regarded as absolutes. Rights-based approaches to problems are in evidence everywhere when we say that the object of human action/interaction to promote, for example, the right to development, the rights of the child, patent rights, the right to health, the right to work, legal and political rights, economic, social and cultural rights, land rights, animal rights, etc.

There was a time when rights and duties were thought of as two sides of the same coin. The paradigm was that every right was supported by a corresponding duty. Citizenship brought with it rights and duties. Although now rights and freedoms have been enshrined as part of the basic laws of Canada through the *Charter of Rights and Freedoms*, what has happened to duties? Have they just disappeared? When was the last time you heard the expression "civic duty"?

The current paradigm (of social and political interaction) is a different one. It is not about rights and corresponding duties but rather about competing rights, the need to first acknowledge where they compete with each other and then work to accommodate the other's rights.

The word duty has almost a quaint musty odour about it. Perhaps it belongs on the shelf with other outmoded notions such as love of country, the three Rs, church attendance, neighbourliness, and the whole big box of ideas, assumptions and institutions labelled the welfare state.

## THREE SETS OF DUTIES

I propose to examine the earlier question — Is duty dead? — by looking at three sets of duties. The first are those found in Part 8 of the Criminal Code of Canada. Failure to perform these will bring into operation the full force of the criminal law with all that implies. The Code sections establish criminal responsibility where someone voluntarily undertakes to do an act, fails to do so and thereby puts another's life in danger, or alternatively is in a relationship where the other is dependent or vulnerable and fails to perform a duty that results in death, injury or permanent danger to health.

Next, in a nod to current events (April 2003) in Iraq, I would like to look at three of the duties that an Occupying Power has to those under its control as found in the Fourth Geneva Convention, which is relative to the Protection of Civilian Persons in Time of War. These are duties found in international humanitarian law which we used to term "soft" law or "gray" as opposed to black-letter law. With the adoption by the Security Council of the United Nations of the Statutes of the International Tribunals for the former Yugoslavia and Rwanda, some "grave breaches" of the Conventions have come in from the gray area of international law into the new black-letter international criminal law. The Statute of the International Tribunal for the former Yugoslavia, for example, criminalizes in Article 2 certain grave breaches of the Geneva Conventions.[1]

Thirdly, I would like to examine the United Nations Millennium Development Goals which, at first glance, one might be hard-pressed to describe as anything but statements of good intentions. Upon further analysis, however, they may have characteristics that mark them as embryonic duties that are moral and eventually just possibly legal. But first, a definition of duty is needed.

## DEFINITION OF DUTY

I manage a large justice sector development programme in Nigeria. To do so, I need to be practical and there is nothing more practical than a good theory. Therefore, Kant, and his *Fundamental Principles of the Metaphysics of Ethics* supplies the definition of what constitutes a duty. For Kant, duty is the necessity of acting from respect for the law and one should follow the law even to the thwarting of all one's inclinations.

Kant acknowledges that

> although respect is a feeling, it is not a feeling received through influence, but is self-wrought by a rational concept, and, therefore, is specifically distinct from all feelings of the former kind, which may be referred either to inclination or fear. What I recognise immediately as a law for me, I recognise with respect.

> This merely signifies the consciousness that my will is subordinate to a law, without the intervention of other influences on my sense. The immediate determination of the will by the law, and the consciousness of this, is called respect, so that this is regarded as an effect of the law on the subject,

and not as the cause of it. Respect is properly the conception of a worth which thwarts my self-love. Accordingly it is something which is considered neither as an object of inclination nor of fear, although it has something analogous to both. The object of respect is the law only, and that the law which we impose on ourselves and yet recognise as necessary in itself. As a law, we are subjected to it without consulting self-love (Kant, 1938).

If we have hitherto drawn our notion of duty from the common use of our practical reason, it is by no means to be inferred that we have treated it as an empirical notion. On the contrary, if we attend to the experience of men's conduct, we meet frequent and, as we ourselves allow, just complaints that one cannot find a single certain example of the disposition to act from pure duty. But that reason of itself, independent on all experience, ordains what ought to take place (ibid., p. 13).

For the pure conception of duty, unmixed with any foreign addition of empirical attractions, and, in a word, the conception of the moral law, exercises on the human heart, by way of reason alone (which first becomes aware with this that it can of itself be practical), an influence so much more powerful than all other springs which may be derived from the field of experience, that, in the consciousness of its worth, it despises the latter, and can by degrees become their master; whereas a mixed ethics, compounded partly of motives drawn from feelings and inclinations, and partly also of conceptions of reason, must make the mind waver between motives which cannot be brought under any principle, which lead to good only by mere accident and very often also to evil (ibid., p. 15).

## THE IMPORTANCE OF DUTY IN PUBLIC POLICY

As possibly appealing as this pure conception of duty might be, we know from experience that only a small number of us have our actions spring from the unadulterated concept of acting in respect of the law. One anecdotal estimate is that only 20 per cent of people obey the law all of the time simply because it is the law. Another 20 per cent seldom observe any law and only when they are almost certain of detection and punishment and the remaining 60 per cent usually base their actions on a mixture of motives, including respect for the law itself but also feelings and inclinations that may lead to "good by accident" but often can produce a different result. Whether these proportions are generally correct or whether they vary according to social groups, the actual law itself or as to the perceived willingness or capacity of the authorities to enforce the law can usefully be examined further. What is important, however, is that there is some proportion of individuals who obey certain laws simply because it is the law. In other words, we behave out of a Kantian sense of duty.

The existence of this group is important because a central problem for policymakers in the field of justice or perhaps any field of government that requires compliance with a law or a policy is how to maximize citizen compliance by regulation or policy at the lowest possible cost. The cost is measured not only in terms of the financial costs of detection, prosecution, the mobilization and presentation of information, then adjudication and, if found culpable, punishment. It also involves costs in incursions on the personal freedom of some or all of us in the search to achieve greater compliance. Governance in this area always involves a constant (re)calculation of the benefits of having us comply with a law or policy as against the costs of doing so.

Like all public policy exercises, the attempt to get maximum compliance at the least cost is attenuated by many limitations. The first stem from our limited capacity to detect and prosecute non-compliance. Limitations in resources invariably lead to targeting of the most likely trangressors or "non-compliers". This is where statistics and statistical profiling comes in. If we were able to distinguish those who will comply with the law out of a strong sense of duty, the universe of likely non-compliers would be reduced.

The second major set of limitations comes from the fact that targeting of likely non-compliers can be politically charged as it involves intrusions on liberty by state authorities. If the weight of these intrusions falls disproportionately on a clearly identifiable group who share some identity-based characteristic such as race or ethnicity, there is a real issue of public policy as to whether the public benefit from targeted enforcement outweighs the resulting stigmatization and prejudice which may build against all members of that group. This is at the core of the debate around racial profiling, especially in policing and law enforcement generally. This important debate is not really taking place, at least in Canada.

## SO THEN "IS DUTY DEAD?"

Having established a definition of duty and argued its importance in the practical business of seeking to enforce laws, I want to turn now to examples and attempt to answer my question.

The three sets of duties have different levels of legal authority. The duties in the Criminal Code of Canada are what is termed hard or black-letter law.[2] The general statement of the law relating to duty is found in Section 217 of the Criminal Code.[3] The section provides that "every one who undertakes to do an act is under a legal duty to do it if an omission to do the act is or may be dangerous to life". The basis of criminal liability under this section then is the undertaking to commit an act, the failure to do so and that failure results in bodily harm or death that is punishable as an offence under the Criminal Code. The Criminal Code and related statutes also contain crimes of "pure" omission where a crime is committed even where no danger or harm is occasioned by the omission.[4] The Criminal Code contains more specific duties of which the failure to perform will attract criminal responsibility. Section 216 deals with undertaking surgical or medical treatment.[5] Section 263 creates criminal liability when a person cuts a hole in ice or creates an excavation and leaves it unguarded.[6]

There is also a series of duties in which the failure to perform will attract criminal responsibility where the person has voluntarily entered into a relationship in which the other to whom the duty is owed is either dependent or vulnerable. Section 215 (1) outlines the duties of a parent, foster parent, guardian or head of family.[7] Section 215 (2) imposes criminal liability where the omission to perform the duty "endangers the life of the person to whom the duty is owed, or causes or is likely to cause the health of that person to be endangered or injured permanently."[8] Section 218 deals with the specific case of abandoning or exposing a child under the age of ten.[9]

Unlike the examples of duties from the Fourth Geneva Convention and the Millennium Development Goals, the failure to perform duties under the Criminal Code of Canada will result in a criminal sanction. In addition to the specific sanctions provided under the sections already mentioned, where a person in failing to perform a legal duty shows wanton or reckless disregard for the lives or safety of other persons, he or she will be deemed to be criminally negligent.[10] Where the criminal negligence results in the death of the other, the maximum penalty upon conviction is life imprisonment.[11] Where it results in bodily harm, ten years.[12]

The duties of an Occupying Power under the Fourth Geneva Convention were termed "soft law" or "gray law" until the creation of the International Tribunals and the International Criminal Court because although they established clear norms for how an Occupying Power should act, there was no easy mechanism to provide for the sanctioning of those who did not observe such norms. Now, where the conduct constitutes a Grave Breach of the Geneva Conventions[13] or a crime against humanity,[14] it can be prosecuted and tried as a criminal act by one of the International Tribunals or the International Criminal Court provided that it was committed within the temporal and geographic jurisdiction of the tribunal or court.

Here, I want to examine three articles of the Fourth Geneva Convention dealing with the duties of an Occupying Power — Article 50, obligations toward children,[15] Article 55 dealing with the duty to provide food and medicines to the occupied population[16] and Article 56, duty to provide hospitals and other medical services.[17] What is the force of law, if any, which underpins these duties? Is there any sanction for omitting to perform them? A threshold question is how any person would be bound by such duties. Part of the response would be that an Occupying Power as a nation that has signed the Geneva Conventions would have voluntarily bound itself to perform the duties contained therein. If an Occupying Power is bound, those serving in its armed forces would also be bound.

Failure to perform these duties generally would not normally attract criminal liability except perhaps before the military tribunals of the Occupying Power if its military code made breaches of such duties offences. The Statutes of the International Tribunals and the International Criminal Court have criminalized the failure to perform such duties in certain cases. Article 2 of the Statute of the Yugoslav Tribunal, for example, has criminalized a failure to perform a duty where the actor exceeded a threshold of criminality by "wilfully caus[ing] great suffering or serious injury to body or health" thereby committing a grave breach of a Geneva Convention. Failure to perform such duties may also be a crime against humanity and punishable under Article 5 of the Statute of the Tribunal if it would be judged to have amounted to an "inhumane act".

Although there are differences between the scheme of duties under the Canadian Criminal Code and the Fourth Geneva Convention, there are also similarities. The first is that an actor voluntarily enters into an act or into a relationship where the other is in some way reliant on the actor performing an action, dependent or otherwise vulnerable. The second, and this is what triggers criminal responsibility, is that the failure to perform the duty results in death or injury to the other in the case of the Canadian Criminal Code provisions or great suffering or serious injury to body or health in the case of the Statute of the International Tribunal. The difference between the two criminal statutes is that under the Canadian Criminal Code the accused will be criminally negligent if he or she has shown through this action or omission a wanton or reckless disregard for the lives or safety of other persons. Under the Statute of the International Tribunal, the individual to be found criminally liable must, by their failure to act, have "wilfully caused great suffering or serious injury to body or health".

Now to the Millennium Development Goals[18] which have been voluntarily subscribed to by nations through the United Nations and by subsequent voluntary pronouncements. At the moment, the Millennium Development Goals would be thought to be statements of good intentions. But do they also constitute duties or at least putative duties? They already have some of the characteristics of duties at law in that there are thresholds or standards of care for each. These have been expressed as targets and indicators. Even though one would search in vain for any mechanism to enforce them and therefore in the Austinian (Austin, 1869) sense they would not in strict terms be duties at law, could they be characterized in the Kantian sense as a duty in that they invite respect for "the law which we impose on ourselves and yet recognise as necessary in itself?"

If individuals and nations voluntarily enter into acts to "eradicate extreme poverty and hunger" and then fail to act so that death or serious injury results should that failure trigger any form of moral or legal responsibility? Should the failure to act trigger a process of accountability in every eventuality or only if the failure either demonstrated a wanton or reckless disregard for the lives or safety of other persons or wilfully caused great suffering or serious injury to body or health of another? These questions may be novel placed in the context of the Millennium Development Goals, but they are not idle ones given popular protest against the harm and injury done to people by the fall-out from economic "globalization".

Is duty dead? The answer to that question may depend on the answer to another: Is community dead? For the duties we owe each other are the sinews of community. If we voluntarily enter into an act, we are duty bound to complete the act, save in exceptional circumstances, if our failure to do so would endanger the life or health of another. If we voluntarily enter into a relationship with another we are duty bound, save in exceptional circumstances, to assist or provide, within our capacity, for that person if the failure to do so would result in death or serious injury or harm. The duties we owe to each other in such circumstances are at the very heart of community that relies on mutuality.

The adoption of the Millennium Development Goals demonstrated that the human impulse to live "in community" is not dead, but very much alive. But how can these shared goals best be realized? Do they need to be legislated into a convention or international statute? Or will it be, at least for a time, sufficient for them to acquire the status of moral norms or "laws" which will so command our respect that we will without threat of coercion comply with them? Or do we need a regime of commands and sanctions to sustain them? We can have "globalization" without duty but we cannot have global community without duties.

So then, is duty dead? My answer is that, if the commitment to global community is genuine,[19] then there is every reason to expect that over time the Millennium Development Goals will evolve from statements of good intentions into moral duties, into obligations under international conventions and then into duties enforceable at law whether as provisions of an international criminal statute or a domestic one. The path has already been traced in, for example, the duties under the Fourth Geneva Convention. Citizen activism will be needed at every step of the way to first embarrass, ginger, then cajole, prod and finally galvanize governments into action.

I would argue that the first step has already been taken. Governments, by adopting the Millennium Development Goals, have voluntarily entered into a relationship with millions of poor people around the world in which they now owe a duty to those who are vulnerable or dependent on them.[20] I would further argue that if they fail to perform those duties and if that failure endangers lives or health permanently, there at least is the beginnings of the basis of liability in law.

If "duty" is dead, it is about to undergo a revival.

## NOTES

I would like to thank my good friend, Ian Alexander, for his, as always, incisive comments on an earlier draft of this text.

1. Article 2. The International Tribunal shall have the power to prosecute persons committing or ordering to be committed grave breaches of the Geneva Conventions of 12 August 1949, namely the following acts against

persons or property protected under the provisions of the relevant Geneva Convention:

(a) wilful killing;

(b) torture or inhuman treatment, including biological experiments;

(c) wilfully causing great suffering or serious injury to body or health;

(d) extensive destruction and appropriation of property, not justified by military necessity and carried out unlawfully and wantonly;

(e) compelling a prisoner of war or a civilian to serve in the forces of a hostile power;

(f) wilfully depriving a prisoner of war or a civilian of the rights of fair and regular trial;

(g) unlawful deportation or transfer or unlawful confinement of a civilian;

(h) taking civilians as hostages.

2. I am indebted to François Lareau, a friend, scholar and dedicated reformer of the Criminal Code of Canada for his insights into these sections of the Code.

3. A "duty imposed by law" for the purpose of section 219(2) on criminal negligence, includes common law duties and statutory duties (*R. v. Coyne* [1958] 124 C.C.C. 176 (N.B.C.A.)). This can go very far, for example, section 2 of the *Quebec Charter of Human Rights and Freedoms*, provides that "every human being whose life is in peril has a right to assistance. Every person must come to the aid of anyone whose life is in peril, either personally or calling for aid, by giving him the necessary and immediate physical assistance, unless it involves danger to himself or a third person, or he has another valid reason."

4. Failing to file a tax return for instance, section 238(1) of the *Income Tax Act*, R.S.C. 1985

5. Section 216 states that every one who undertakes to administer surgical or medical treatment to another person or to do any other lawful act that may endanger the life of another person is, except in cases of necessity, under a legal duty to have and to use reasonable knowledge, skill and care in so doing.

6. Section 263.

(1) Every one who makes or causes to be made an opening in ice that is open to or frequented by the public is under a legal duty to guard it in a manner that is adequate to prevent persons from falling in by accident and is adequate to warn them that the opening exists.

(2) Every one who leaves an excavation on land that he owns or of which he has charge or supervision is under a legal duty to guard it in a manner

that is adequate to prevent persons from falling in by accident and is adequate to warn them that the excavation exists.

(3) Every one who fails to perform a duty imposed by subsection (1) or (2) is guilty of

   (*a*) manslaughter, if the death of any person results therefrom;

   (*b*) an offence under section 269, if bodily harm to any person results therefrom; or

   (*c*) an offence punishable on summary conviction.

7.  Section 215.

(1) Every one is under a legal duty

   (*a*) as a parent, foster parent, guardian or head of a family, to provide necessaries of life for a child under the age of sixteen years;

   (*b*) to provide necessaries of life to their spouse or common-law partner; and

   (*c*) to provide necessaries of life to a person under his charge if that person

      (i) is unable, by reason of detention, age, illness, mental disorder or other cause, to withdraw himself from that charge, and

      (ii) is unable to provide himself with necessaries of life.

8.  Section 215.

(2) Every one commits an offence who, being under a legal duty within the meaning of subsection (1), fails without lawful excuse, the proof of which lies upon him, to perform that duty, if

   (*a*) with respect to a duty imposed by paragraph (1)(*a*) or (*b*),

      (i) the person to whom the duty is owed is in destitute or necessitous circumstances, or

      (ii) the failure to perform the duty endangers the life of the person to whom the duty is owed, or causes or is likely to cause the health of that person to be endangered permanently; or

   (*b*) with respect to a duty imposed by paragraph (1)(*c*), the failure to perform the duty endangers the life of the person to whom the duty is owed or causes or is likely to cause the health of that person to be injured permanently.

9.  Section 218. Every one who unlawfully abandons or exposes a child who is under the age of ten years, so that its life is or is likely to be endangered or its health is or is likely to be permanently injured, is guilty of an indictable offence and liable to imprisonment for a term not exceeding two years.

10. Section 219.

(1) Every one is criminally negligent who

    (*a*) in doing anything, or

    (*b*) in omitting to do anything that it is his duty to do, shows wanton or reckless disregard for the lives or safety of other persons.

(2) For the purposes of this section, "duty" means a duty imposed by law.

11. Section 220. Every person who by criminal negligence causes death to another person is guilty of an indictable offence and liable

    (*a*) where a firearm is used in the commission of the offence, to imprisonment for life and to a minimum punishment of imprisonment for a term of four years; and

    (*b*) in any other case, to imprisonment for life.

12. Section 221. Every one who by criminal negligence causes bodily harm to another person is guilty of an indictable offence and liable to imprisonment for a term not exceeding ten years.

13. See note 8 as an example in the case of the Yugoslav Tribunal.

14. For example, again, the Statute of the Yugoslav Tribunal,

Article 5, Crimes against humanity

The International Tribunal shall have the power to prosecute persons responsible for the following crimes when committed in armed conflict, whether international or internal in character, and directed against any civilian population:

    (a) murder;

    (b) extermination;

    (c) enslavement;

    (d) deportation;

    (e) imprisonment;

    (f) torture;

    (g) rape;

    (h) persecutions on political, racial and religious grounds;

    (i) other inhumane acts.

15. Article 50. The Occupying Power shall, with the co-operation of the national and local authorities, facilitate the proper working of all institutions devoted to the care and education of children.

The Occupying Power shall take all necessary steps to facilitate the identification of children and the registration of their parentage. It may not, in any case, change their personal status, nor enlist them in formations or organizations subordinate to it.

Should the local institutions be inadequate for the purpose, the Occupying Power shall make arrangements for the maintenance and education, if possible by persons of their own nationality, language and religion, of children who are orphaned or separated from their parents as a result of the war and who cannot be adequately cared for by a near relative or friend.

A special section of the Bureau set up in accordance with Article 136 shall be responsible for taking all necessary steps to identify children whose identity is in doubt. Particulars of their parents or other near relatives should always be recorded if available.

The Occupying Power shall not hinder the application of any preferential measures in regard to food, medical care and protection against the effects of war which may have been adopted prior to the occupation in favour of children under fifteen years, expectant mothers, and mothers of children under seven years.

16. Article 55. To the fullest extent of the means available to it, the Occupying Power has the duty of ensuring the food and medical supplies of the population; it should, in particular, bring in the necessary foodstuffs, medical stores and other articles if the resources of the occupied territory are inadequate.

    The Occupying Power may not requisition foodstuffs, articles or medical supplies available in the occupied territory, except for use by the occupation forces and administration personnel, and then only if the requirements of the civilian population have been taken into account. Subject to the provisions of other international Conventions, the Occupying Power shall make arrangements to ensure that fair value is paid for any requisitioned goods.

    The Protecting Power shall, at any time, be at liberty to verify the state of the food and medical supplies in occupied territories, except where temporary restrictions are made necessary by imperative military requirements.

17. Article 56. To the fullest extent of the means available to it, the Occupying Power has the duty of ensuring and maintaining, with the co-operation of national and local authorities, the medical and hospital establishments and services, public health and hygiene in the occupied territory, with particular reference to the adoption and application of the prophylactic and preventive measures necessary to combat the spread of contagious diseases and epidemics. Medical personnel of all categories shall be allowed to carry out their duties.

18. Millennium Development Goals Including Targets and Indicators for Goal 1. For example,

    1. Eradicate extreme poverty and hunger

       Target 1: Halve, between 1990 and 2015, the proportion of people whose income is less than $1 a day

(1a)  Proportion of population below $1 a day

(1b)  National poverty headcount ratio

(2)   Poverty gap ratio at $1 a day *(incidence x depth of poverty)*

(3)   Share of poorest quintile in national consumption

Target 2: Halve, between 1990 and 2015, the proportion of people who suffer from hunger

(4)   Prevalence of underweight in children (under five years of age)

(5)   Proportion of population below minimum level of dietary energy consumption

2. Achieve universal primary education

3. Promote gender equality and empower women

4. Reduce child mortality

5. Improve maternal health

6. Combat HIV/AIDS, malaria and other diseases

7. Ensure environmental sustainability

8. Develop a global partnership for development

19. If it is genuine, would it not then give rise to a "moral law" of reciprocal assistance?

20. A good friend, Patti Whaley, although agreeing that the Millennium Development Goals (MDGs) could form the basis of moral duties *if voluntarily entered into* questions whether one can characterize governments' adoption of MDGs as "voluntary" if their motivation for adopting them was not a genuine recognition of reciprocal duties but rather moral guilt of the rich in the face of the plight of the poor. I would argue that absent evidence that the MDGs were entered into under "duress", they were entered into voluntarily and therefore can form the basis, at a minimum, of moral duties.

## REFERENCES

Austin, J. (1869), *Lectures on Jurisprudence, or, The Philosophy of Positive Law*, 3d ed. London: John Murray.

Kant, I. (1938), *The Fundamental Principles of the Metaphysics of Ethics*, trans. O. Manthey-Zom. New York and London: D. Appleton-Century Co.

CHAPTER 23

# Crime Statistics and Behaviour

## D.J. Hand

### INTRODUCTION

Recently, I was vaguely following a television report on the progress of the American forces in Iraq and I was startled to hear the newsreader say that "the police have lost control of the streets of London". My first thought was that the Americans must have advanced faster than expected. But then I realized that the subject matter had changed, and that it was a statement about crime in Britain's capital.

Those who have direct knowledge of crime will almost certainly have that knowledge from just one side, that of the victim. On the other hand, everyone has a substantial amount of indirect knowledge: the news media seem to subsist on a diet that includes crime in a large part; so regurgitated crime is something that is a constant part of every broadcast. It is also something that attracts a certain statistical controversy.

There are various difficulties associated with measuring crime. They include:

- the fact that legislation, and hence what constitutes crime, changes over time and space. It is the difference between legal systems in different parts of the world that makes meaningful international comparisons of crime rates so difficult;
- the fact that the reporting of crime is influenced by perceptions on what might be achieved by reporting it, as well as by such things as social attitudes to victims. By no means is all crime reported;

– the fact that there are also various feedback mechanisms. Before capital punishment was abolished in the United Kingdom, juries were hesitant to reach a verdict of guilty of murder, since it was then mandatory for judges to sentence the perpetrator to death.
– the fact that, if police "productivity" is based on a particular measure, then inevitably recording practices will evolve to maximize apparent performance.

In Britain, information on the extent of crime now comes mainly from two complementary sources: the annual *Crime in England and Wales* reports, collated from police statistics, and the *British Crime Survey* (BCS), a survey of the public. Influences of the kind mentioned mean that the trends apparent from these two sources may not be in the same direction, and this confuses the public. For example, "violent crime appears to be rising according to police statistics, but when one takes into account recording changes, this increase appears to be much smaller, and for those violent crimes reported to the BCS the trend over the past half decade has been down, and significantly so" (Simmons *et al.*, 2002, p. 1).

Slightly under 50 per cent of BCS incidents are reported to the police, and of those reported only about 60 per cent are recorded. Of course, these are aggregate statistics, and they differ between different types of crime. Reasons for not reporting a crime include the feeling that it was too trivial, or that the police could not do anything, or that the victims could deal with it themselves. Complications about recording reported crimes arise from crimes involving multiple victims, as well as changing regulations on what types of crime should be described in the police statistics.

Since 1995, the BCS has reported a fall in crime year on year, with an overall reduction of 22 per cent between 1997 and 2002, with the apparent 7 per cent increase in recorded crime in police statistics being largely attributable to changes in recording practice. I also note, because I shall return to it later, that "the number of detections in 2001–2002 rose slightly on the previous year, by 2 per cent, to 1,290,195 with increases for all crime types except fraud and forgery" (Simmons *et al.*, 2002, p. 4).

Perception of crime is even more difficult to measure than the actual crime rate. In part this is because crime is a relatively well-defined concept, which may not perfectly match what is perceived as morally wrong. We have an offence of criminal damage, which may not coincide with what is perceived as damage by any individual. To be a crime, an action has to be so classified by the legal system. For example, causing someone to die may or may not be murder, depending on the circumstances, but a relative of the victim may not be inclined to make much of a distinction. In the context of perception of crime, Simmons *et al.* remark that "readers of the national tabloid papers are much more likely to consider the national crime rate to have increased over this period, compared to broadsheet readers (42 per cent *versus* 26 per cent)" (ibid.).

The relationship between crime and morality is also elegantly illustrated by the success of the policy of zero tolerance. If some minor social infringement is ignored and allowed to pass, then the perpetrator is encouraged to commit larger insults. Where does one draw the line? The zero-tolerance policy spells out that line explicitly, shifting the onus of deciding where to draw the line away from the individual. It articulates social morality in order that the individual does not have to make a choice.

The problems associated with measuring crime are both challenging and fascinating. However, although it is an area of great technical interest, these problems are probably better discussed in a specialist statistics conference. Moreover, the relationship between crime and morality would lead us into the realms of jurisprudence, and I know too little of that to say anything of value in the context of measuring crime. I want to shift attention to an issue that more closely intertwines crime and morality and which, rather to my surprise, threatens to have an impact on my own work.

## DATA MINING

The aim of data mining is the discovery of interesting, unexpected, or valuable structures in large datasets. "Sounds like statistics", you might say, and it does have considerable overlap with statistics. It differs in emphasis, however, and this has bearing on the ethical and moral issues.

I find it useful to split data mining into two domains: that concerned with modelling and that concerned with what I shall call pattern detection (see, e.g., Hand, Mannila and Smyth, 2001). My interest here lies with the latter.

Pattern detection is concerned with detecting local anomalies: small groups of cases or small locations in the space of the data which appear to behave in an unexpected way relative to the mass of data. Unlike modelling, pattern detection is not aimed at decomposing an entire set of data, but focuses on small regions. Here are a couple of examples of patterns: simultaneous use of a credit card in two different geographical locations suggests fraud; repeated attempts to log onto the same computer using different incorrect passwords suggests a hacking attempt. More elaborate examples are readily found.

Now, of course, some areas of statistics are concerned with discovering and locating such anomalous behaviours. Three such areas spring to mind: outlier detection, disease clustering in epidemiology and scan statistics. However, these are typically concerned with single points (outliers), or with only two or three dimensions (epidemiology), or with restricted forms of assumed background distribution, relative to the anomaly sought (scan statistics). Pattern detection in data mining is generally faced with very large sets of data, in many dimensions and possibly with undefined background distributions.

Pattern detection has very obvious applications in crime detection. One is essentially seeking people or groups of people who behave in an unusual way, either relative to other people or relative to how they have behaved in the past. Note that I am talking about detection rather than prevention, although detecting that someone has committed a crime may lead to preventing them from committing any more. Examples include individuals serving as a nexus of phone calls that includes known criminals, credit-card purchases of multiple items that can easily be sold, DNA matching, and so on.

Of course, discovering such people or groups is not a proof that they are behaving illegally, but one can then focus one's investigative resources on such cases, rather than spreading them thinly on cases that appear to be behaving in a perfectly normal way. The role of pattern detection in fraud is described in Bolton and Hand (2002).

This sort of application, constantly monitoring people to detect out of the ordinary behaviour, has recently become topical in another criminal arena: that of detecting potential terrorist threats, especially, of course, in the United States. Here are two examples, the first relating to airline passengers:

> In the US Transportation Security Administration's (TSA) *Computer Assisted Passenger Profiling System (CAPPS II)*, passengers give their name, address, phone number, and date of birth, and this information allows airline reservation systems to automatically obtain a background check from

the TSA which includes credit, banking history, and a criminal background check ... A colour coded risk assessment is then encrypted onto the passenger's boarding pass. A red assessment will prevent the passenger from flying (Mark, 2003).

The next quotation is from a description of the United States DARPA project's Total information awareness project:

The Defense Advanced Research Projects Agency's (DARPA) mission is to research and demonstrate innovative technologies to solve national-level problems, such as the grave terrorist threat which our nation faces. DARPA created the Information Awareness Office (IAO) in response to September 11, 2001, to research, develop, and demonstrate innovative information technologies to detect terrorist groups planning attacks against American citizens, anywhere in the world.... IAO is developing an experimental prototype system that consists of three parts — language translation technologies, data search and pattern recognition technologies, and advanced collaborative and decision support tools.... The research into data search and pattern recognition technologies is based on the idea that terrorist planning activities or a likely terrorist attack could be uncovered by searching for indications of terrorist activities in vast quantities of transaction data. Terrorists must engage in certain transactions to coordinate and conduct attacks against Americans, and these transactions form patterns that may be detectable (DARPA: Information Awareness Office).

These schemes are fine in principle, but have some major technical hurdles to overcome. One of them, just as an illustration, is the problem arising from unbalanced classes: the number of terrorists in the United States is far smaller than the number of non-terrorists. Even if the system correctly identifies 99 per cent of the terrorists as terrorists, and 99 per cent of the non-terrorists as non-terrorists, the fact that there are so many more non-terrorists than terrorists means that almost all of those identified are innocent.

More is at stake than the technical aspects, however. In particular, civil liberties organizations are becoming increasingly concerned about the intensive invasion of privacy such systems imply. There are obvious commercial gains to be had from deep knowledge about customers and potential customers.

The TIA [Total Information Awareness] program, under the direction of the Defense Advanced Research Projects Agency (DARPA), aims to capture the "information signature" of people in order to track potential terrorists and has been sharply criticized by privacy and civil liberties advocates. Congress is currently blocking funding for the program because of privacy concerns (Mark, 2003).

I do not think I am too concerned about that sort of issue. I think it would be a good idea if there were a national DNA data-bank: the clear-up rate for crime would dwarf those in the previous discussion. Furthermore, we have seen several high-profile cases in recent years of innocents being released from prison after DNA matches showed that they could not have committed the crime. However, unfortunately, and as so often happens, there is a knock-on effect from the adverse publicity which the TIA program is attracting. *Data mining* as a whole is now being tarred with the same brush as the TIA program. The technology, rather than the application, is being criticized. It means, to take some concrete examples, that my work on patterns in genome sequences, on locating faults in large complex systems such as telecom networks, and in identifying students who have plagiarized their reports is at risk.

This development has stimulated the Executive Committee of the Association for Computing Machinery Special Interest Group on Knowledge Discovery and Data Mining (February 20, 2003) to make a formal statement:

> Some of the people who are not knowledgeable about data mining technology are apparently equating data mining technology to guaranteed violation of civil liberties.... We believe that the debate about technology's potential for violating civil liberties should be focused solely on the misuse of stored data, not on anything else — not on data mining technology, database management technology, the Internet, or even the creation of a national database as envisioned by the TIA initiative.

## CONCLUSION

We are back to what appears to be the central theme, the issue of whether science is amoral, and the extent to which individual scientists should take responsibility for the use to which their inventions and discoveries are put. Data-mining technology, as a case in point, has a vast potential for human good, *via* its applications in medicine and other areas. In my view it would be a tremendously retrograde step to ban it on the spurious grounds that it can also be used for the bad. To do so would represent Luddism of the most extreme kind. It would also probably be doomed to fail.

*Epilogue*: Subsequent to my giving this talk, the name "Total Information Awareness" program was changed to "Terrorist Information Awareness" program, preserving the acronym but shifting attention to non-US nationals.

## REFERENCES

Bolton, R.J. and Hand, D.J. (2002), "Statistical Fraud Detection: A Review", *Statistical Science* 17:235-255.

Hand, D.J., Mannila, H. and Smyth, P. (2001), *Principles of Data Mining*. Cambridge, MA: MIT Press.

Mark, R. (2003), "TSA Books Data Mining Program", *dc.internet.com*, March 4. At <http://www.internet.com>.

Simmons, J. *et al.* (2002), *Crime in England and Wales 2001/2*. London: The Home Office.

CHAPTER 24

# Fact and Science Fiction: The Ethical and Legal Challenge

J.S.C. McKee

## INTRODUCTION

In 1627, an important historical event occurred with the birth of Robert Boyle, now generally regarded as the originator of the scientific method. In particular it was the synergism between Robert Boyle and Robert Hooke that finally pointed the way toward the establishment of scientific fact. Boyle's research into the physics of gases owed much of its success to the invention of the air-pump. Indeed, the pump which he used in his research was the most sophisticated of its kind in operation. It was, however, susceptible to technical failure and only the good offices of Robert Hooke, the curator of experiments for the Royal Society, and his genius as an experimental scientist enabled this pioneering work to be completed. Thus, Robert Boyle, anxious to establish the validity of his observations, wrote up in great detail the conditions under which all measurements were made and the nature of his experimental technique. In this way he ensured that others with similar or different equipment could repeat and confirm his already completed experiments. The scientific method was born of technical necessity rather than philosophical ideology. Since then, the scientific method has maintained its fundamental position at the heart of the search for scientific truth, and given scientists a yardstick against which to measure their results. But all that may be changing. There is a less than subtle change of emphasis when we look at recent definitions of the scientific method. We now read that the scientific method, once considered a rigorous procedure that included the study of scientific hypotheses, induction, theories, laws and methods of explanation, is now regarded as a family of methods each of which differs according to the subject matter involved. The core of the scientific method, however it is defined, is still related to the measurement of phenomena and experimentation or repeated observations.

Nonetheless, now, in 2003, the scientific method seems no longer to be considered a monolithic and rigorous procedure. Indeed, it seems that it may vary, both according to the subject and the discipline concerned. If so, what does this imply in the search for scientific truth and fact, and, are fact and fiction still distinguishable?

## PATHOLOGICAL, PRECAUTIONARY AND CONSENSUS SCIENCE

### Pathological Science

In recent years, much has been heard of three variants to the normal ways of identifying scientific fact. Although all three have their limitations, by far the most alarming is pathological science, a disease that is much more widespread than anyone might previously have deemed possible. It is a variant of normal scientific study and was first identified by Irving Langmuir in 1953. Although there are many widely documented cases of pathological research, the works of Barnes (1930) and Davis and Barnes (1931) on Balmer rays; that of Blondlot (1905) on N-rays, and that of Gurwitsch (see Langmuir 1989) on mitogenic rays, are at the forefront of such research. Indeed, the fact that so many scientists the world over initially produced confirmatory evidence for these phenomena must be of continuing concern to any responsible scientist. Of course, the most recent manifestation of pathological research lies in the cold fusion debacle. Douglas Morrison has analyzed the global response to the Pons and Fleischmann discovery in terms of the Langmuir criteria. He suggests that cold fusion is a classic case of pathological science (Morrison, 1990).

According to Morrison, there are three phases of discovery in pathological science: the first is when a number is quickly confirmed by other workers, a second in which equal numbers of positive and negative results appear, and a third containing an avalanche of negative results. The cold fusion saga exactly fits this mould. He also notes that in many such cases the experimental results obtained seem to be influenced by local community desire which is of concern to objective scientists in all disciplines. In summary, the fact that pathological science is still alive and well should promote healthy scepticism in all of us when examining new scientific data.

## Precautionary Science

The evolution of precautionary science is a rather new phenomenon. In this field remedial action is recommended in the environmental science area despite the absence of an established causal relationship between an environmental effect and some form of human activity. In the absence of scientific knowledge or of models that predict an effect it appears unscientific to recommend redress or a solution to the problem. Society has adopted the contrary view and various articles on the subject have recently appeared in the scientific literature. The point about precautionary science is that it is not science, it is merely prudence. On the other hand, no scientist would insist that all political or social action should depend upon the establishment of scientific discovery or fact. When it is known that an environment is harmful to the human organism, every effort should be made at the local level to improve it — after all, the great strides taken recently in rehabilitating the industrial towns of Europe owe little to current fears of global warming and much to a concern for the future health of its citizens.

Precautionary science, whatever else it may be, is not a science. It advocates action in the absence of scientific fact. This may be prudence, but it is certainly not science. The development of precautionary science should be watched carefully.

## Consensus Science

Consensus science, on the other hand, goes one step further. It states that in the absence of hard scientific fact or causal relationships, a majority vote of scientists can determine scientific truth. This is a new concept for science. For example, it was recently announced that there was a consensus among 300 scientists that global warming could be 1 to 8° C by the year 2030. When scientific proof is absent, consensus has taken over and positive action is recommended. Is scientific fact then no longer necessary, and is it now more acceptable to take decisions in the real world on the basis of "hunches" and "gut reactions" than causal scientific relationships? Why pursue knowledge if society neither wants nor needs it?

Perhaps the scientific revolution is over, and the need for science gone. The prospects are alarming.

## SCIENTIFIC FICTION

It is supposed to be difficult to fool all of the people all of the time, but when most of the scientists you know have been completely bamboozled by pseudo-scientific papers, and may even testify to their veracity long after their discreditation, some doubts arise about that thesis.

Perhaps no fictional science has attracted more attention and affection than the excellent paper submitted to *Physical Review Letters* by Professor J. H. Hetherington and his cat. This story is simple and straightforward. Hetherington, a physicist at Michigan State University, had completed an excellent piece of work on atomic exchange effects in $bcc^3He$. It was to be submitted for rapid publication and a senior member of the Physics Department at East Lansing was invited to read it before transmission to the journal. The editor commented that although it was a fine piece of work it could not be accepted because there was only one author (Hetherington) whereas the Royal "we" was used throughout in describing the work and its results. The paper, it was clear, could be rejected, not on the basis of the physics but on the basis of style. It was suggested that either Hetherington rewrite the paper, a major task, or add a co-author, perhaps a graduate student who had been associated with the work.

Well, there was no student, but that evening, so the story goes, Hetherington's eye fell on his cat Chester, son of Willard, who immediately became his co-author. To add authenticity, the initials F. D. were added — short for *felix domesticus* or domestic cat, and F.D.C. Willard, the world's first feline physicist, rushed into print. Perhaps this fiction would never have come to the public eye had not Willard seen fit to sign reprints of the article with an inky paw before sending them to other colleagues in the field. Such reprints are now regarded with great esteem by many, including the staff at the National Science Foundation, the funding agency that sponsored Hetherington's work. Further details of this calumny have been published elsewhere and make good reading; see Hetherington and Willard (1975).

Probably no unit is more widely used in chemistry than the litre, yet relatively little is known about the eighteenth-century maker of wine bottles, Claude Émile Jean-Baptiste Litre. He first proposed the system of specifying volumes in terms of the mass of liquid that a container would hold. He was the pre-eminent manufacturer of chemical glass-ware of his day, the first to produce precision-graduated cylinders and the inventor of the burette. His graduated cylinders varied in internal diameter by less than 0.1 per cent of their length, and were graduated into hundredths, or even thousandths, of their volume.

Unfortunately for historians, Litre did not keep a journal of his work or his personal life, and any letters exchanged with his close friend Celsius have been lost. His fine glassware has not survived. A set of graduated cylinders donated to the Royal Society of England in 1765 were destroyed 47 years later during the preparation of nitrogen trichlo-ride by Sir Humphrey Davy.

Most details of Litre's life were inferred from the general literature of the period, and it reveals that Litre, unlike most chemists of his generation, enjoyed prosperity, good health and recognition during his lifetime. He was hard-working, but abstained from excesses, and had a placid composure. But then, Litre was not really a chemist. He was a manufacturer of wine bottles, as was his father, grandfather and great-grandfather. His family's wine bottles were well-known in the Bordeaux wine industry since the 1620s. No doubt, this family tradition of glass-working was a major influence when Litre began his scientific training at the age of sixteen. So, too, was his meeting with Anders Celsius four years later during a geological expedition to the Swedish Lapland.

– – –

In 1763 at the age of 47, Litre prepared his major written work, *Etudes Volumetriques*. He chose a standard volume very close to the *flacon royal*, introduced by King Henri IV in 1595 to standardize taxa-tion of wine. However, Litre recognized that this unit was arbitrary, and suggested that volumes be specified in terms of the mass of stand-ard liquid that a container would hold.

– – –

Two hundred years after Litre's death, the litre was adopted as the fundamental unit of volume for the standardized international SI met-ric system (Systéme International). The fact that this account of Litre's life is a pure fabrication was not revealed until three years later by which time it was much too late to avoid dissemination of the biogra-phy to a significant number of gullible readers worldwide. Indeed this account of Litre's life has since appeared in public school materials in

Canada, and has acquired, as it were, a life of its own. When Professor M.L. McGlashan of University College London finally drew the attention of the editors of *Chemistry International* (1980), the journal of publication of the article, to the hoax, he said that he found it almost unbelievable that so many otherwise reputable scientists could swallow such an article. It appears indeed that many scientists initially refused to listen to McGlashan. Eventually, however, the editors published an apology for printing, as legitimate, an article which on further consideration could have been identified as a spoof. This saga is now ended, but the mythology lingers on.

## REFERENCES

Barnes, A.H. (1930), "Capture of Electrons by Alpha-Particles", *Physical Review* 35(3):217-228.

Davis, B. and Barnes, A.H. (1931), "The Molecular Scattering of Light from Ammonia Solutions", Letter, *Physical Review* 37:1368.

Blondlot, R. (1905), *The N-Rays*. London: Longmans, Green and *Encyclopedia Britannica*.

"Chemical History is Shaped by a Maker of Wine Bottles", (1980), Editorial, *Chemistry International* (1):32.

Hetherington, J.H. and Willard, F.D.C. (1975). "Two, Three-, and Four-Atom Exchange Effects in bcc$^3$He", Letter, *Physical Review* 35:1442-1444. (See *More Random Walks in Science*. An anthology compiled by R.L. Weber. Bristol: The Institute of Physics 1982, pp. 110-111.)

Langmuir, I. (1989), "Pathological Science", *Physics Today* (October):36-48.

Morrison, D.R.O. (1990), "The Cold Fusion Confusion". At <CERN/PPE/ 5002 R/DROM/gm>.

# PART IX

## TRUTH *VERSUS* JUSTICE

CHAPTER 25

# Truth *versus* Justice: No Contest?

J.M. Spence

The invitation (or challenge) to address the topic of "Truth *versus* Justice" offered a temptation to engage in abstract speculation, a temptation that will not be entirely resisted in the comments that follow. The topic as stated is also notable for its apparent assertion of some inherent or inevitable opposition between truth and justice. This suggests a certifiably post-modern perspective. In an effort to accommodate that perspective, I have added to the topic the interrogative suffix "No Contest?" in the hope of deferring resolution, at least for a while.

That truth and justice might in some fundamental way be mutually contradictory seems, in the first place, hard to credit. Our more natural inclination is to say rather that it is because we can know the truth that we can do justice. One need only consider, for example, the discovery of DNA (deoxyribonucleic acid) and the beneficial effect it has had on the criminal justice system.

If truth and justice are somehow basically opposed, that would also seem to be a profound counsel of despair about human prospects. That would be so if what is meant is that even if we can know truth in certain respects, we do not and cannot have the means to do so in order to accomplish justice. From this perspective, the contention would be that the beneficial effect of DNA on the justice system, far from being instructive and promising, is rather the atypical exception that proves a profoundly discouraging rule.

It is not at all clear how we would come to judgement about such a dismal proposition. It expresses a vision that is pure and dark but, in its vast altitude, the air is thin. With ordinary human work at hand, we necessarily tell ourselves that we must try to do our best and we cannot do more.

I do not mean to espouse a comfortable presumption about our access to truth and justice. We are long past a time of imperial certitudes. We hear with an appropriately ironic attitude the student doggerel from Victorian Oxford:

> My name is Benjamin Jowett
> I am the Master of Balliol College
> Whatever is known I know it
> What I don't know is not Knowledge.

More than a century later, after previously unimaginable scientific exploits and discoveries and radical developments in public order, we are properly suspicious of claims that assert a foundational stature. In science, even scorning continental fancies about science as a social construct and leaving aside whatever we might think of the idea of paradigm shifts, we recognize that so much that is of value is also provisional. And we are aware that justice, the profound and ancient demand, is also a concept so contentious in light of social science and historical studies and jurisprudential disputes as to be inherently problematic.

All of these developments leave us with an inheritance of skepticism about both truth and justice. Even so, acting responsibly, we may regard this skepticism not only as a burden but also as a device, a tool for our labours.

From such a perspective, we can see a different relationship between truth and justice: not that of contraries but of complementaries. As mentioned, there is no justice without truth. To act justly, to do justice, we have to have the facts. And there is a mutuality to this complementary relationship, for, to have the facts, we must make a sound assessment of the relevant considerations, we must make an appraisal that is adequate to those considerations, that is, in a word, *just.*

A better working hypothesis may be "the more truth, the more justice". But this desirable optimal condition is not to be realized automatically. To bring truth to bear in the cause of justice we are obliged to look to the work of the law. Following this line of thought, we can say that if we are to be able to do justice through the law we must have conditions in the institutions of the justice system that allow the truth to be found. The justice system that we have inherited and employ enshrines two cardinal features to ensure that the conditions for the discovery and reception of the truth operate effectively: one is that each party to the dispute has a full opportunity to test the position of the other and the second is that the decision is taken by a person who is impartial as between the parties and their dispute.

Of course, to state these two essentials is also to open the door to the continuing argument about how well these features are being implemented.

I say the continuing argument over these matters, although it is not always apparent that such an argument is under way in matters relating to the law and the courts. Another story from Victorian times is that for the celebration of the jubilee of Queen Victoria, the judges of the highest courts of England proposed to express their collective congratulations but fell into dispute over the appropriately respectful preamble. The main proposal was to begin with the phrase "Your Majesty's Justices, mindful as we are of our shortcomings..." but one judge objected that, were he mindful of shortcomings, he should feel obliged to resign his judicial office. Another judge helpfully recommended the alternative formulation: "mindful as we are of one another's shortcomings".

These days we are mindful of a vast host of shortcomings that are often at hand in the work of the justice system. These include, with regard to truth, such matters as the sensitive difficulties of assessing credibility in a multicultural society and the constant mushrooming of areas of expertise. The story is told that, in a British Columbia court, expert evidence was proffered and admitted on the subject of falling off ladders. Someone not schooled in the proper manners of a pluralist society had the nerve to say the expert was an Irishman. Well, perhaps that was just a joke, but I can certainly imagine circumstances where such expert evidence could be relevant and admissible. You might suppose that such expert evidence is another example of "junk science" in the courtroom, but how is the judge to be sure? The judge will have to decide if the evidence is admissible and if it is the question then will be how much weight to give to it. Frequently the trier of fact is a jury of people with no particular educational qualifications. Where the trier of fact is a judge, it is quite likely that the judge will have no specialist background in the area under consideration.

That may be just as well: judges who have a little knowledge in a particular area know how that can, in the old adage, be a dangerous thing. But the increasing pace of the information explosion means that these concerns will not disappear.

The question of what counts as proper subject matter for expert evidence continues to claim great attention within the justice system. The problem of experts who are really champions for their clients rather than impartial consultants for the court persists. Ideas for greater use of court-appointed experts are given serious discussion. And at the level of the structure of the justice system and administrative tribunals, the use of expert panels as the decisionmakers becomes more commonplace.

Truth pertains not only to facts but also to understanding. We properly speak of achieving a true understanding of a subject: that is, of coming to an adequate and reliable perception of its elements and their configuration. Attending in this way we might discern a different significance in what many disparage as the triumph of relativism. Truth, we might say, has not been demolished, it has instead been revealed as manifold. We learn to see what was invisible before, truth is found to have new and different dimensions and the ancient demand for justice yields novel claims. Or so I infer, reflecting on my recent experience judging a moot court. The law students were disputing a case under our *Charter of Rights and Freedoms*. It concerned a hypothetical Canadian government foreign-service regulation eliminating female volunteer youth intern employment positions for Canadians in certain African countries. The reason for the regulation was that in those countries female interns had been the victims of sexual violence. The issue was whether this regulation, intended for the protection of women, illegally discriminated against women.

All four of the law students in the moot court were women. Most of the people in the courtroom were women. This may not seem exceptional today but it would have been so forty years ago. Then there were very few women in law school. Nor was there a Charter. In this ordinary prosaic event there is a little illustration of the interaction of law and social change. New law, new facts, new understandings; so, in terms of our topic: new truth and new justice.

With these considerations in mind, we might posit another troubling meaning for the topic of truth *versus* justice: too much truth for the justice system to bear. But just as other pessimistic assessments of the relationship between truth and justice more properly leave us perturbed but not convinced, so this one also suggests not so much an inevitable outcome as a challenge. It is a challenge that all those concerned with truth and justice will expect all of us in the justice system to address, by doing the best we can. What counts as justice may seem more problematic now than in more settled eras of the past, but we are unlikely to quarrel with Aristotle when he writes about justice: that neither the evening star nor the morning star is more glorious.

# PART X

## GENES, ETHICS AND SCIENCE

CHAPTER 26

# A Horror Story: Somatic Nuclear-Cell Transfer Meets Canadian Parliamentary Procedures

P. Calamai

In 1989, the Canadian government set up the Royal Commission on New Reproductive Technology, largely spurred by having to deal with unregulated fertility clinics, but also because of assisted human reproduction. After some stormy years, the commission reported in 1993 that there was a pressing need for action in the emerging field of experimentation with human embryos and with cloning, both reproductive and therapeutic.

Since then Dolly, the sheep, and at least eight other species have been cloned. There has been a flurry of news reports about cloning humans. The human genome has been mapped. Also, ten years after the Royal Commission on New Reproductive Technology reported, the Canadian Parliament has finally come within shooting distance of passing Bill C-13, the legislation arising from the commission's recommendations. After passage, proclamation and Royal Assent, this will become an act respecting assisted human reproductive technologies and related research.

One provision of this legislation effectively bans somatic nuclear-cell transfer, which I am going to call therapeutic cloning. This involves removing the nucleus of an unfertilized human egg, replacing it with material from a donor's somatic cells (skin, heart, nerve cells). Then the egg cells are stimulated and begin dividing. Some five or six days later embryonic stem cells are extracted and can be used for further research. Obviously, extracting those embryonic stem cells kills the embryo. The promise is that these pluri-potent embryonic stem cells can be introduced into areas of the donor's body where organs are damaged. It is presumed that healthy tissue of different types will then regrow. This approach is especially promising for diseases like diabetes, Parkinson's and Alzheimer's. Since the somatic cells originated with the donor, the patient into whom the tissue is transplanted should not have a rejection problem.

Many scientists are far from certain that this technology will ever produce anything of therapeutic value. As a working group organized by the Canadian Institutes of Health Research states in a discussion paper:

> The efficiency of somatic cell nuclear transfer is very low, even in non-human mammals, and the normal development of embryos and cell lines derived in this manner is uncertain. How nuclear transfer reprograms the nuclear DNA, as well as how this knowledge might be applied to stem cell research, is currently best explained in non-human systems. Furthermore, many basic issues of the therapeutic potential of human ES cells need to be explored before any possible direct application of nuclear transfer technology could be envisaged (CIHR, 2001).

Thus a great big flashing caution sign was erected at the beginning of this process. This is probably good because any researcher in Canada who wants to try therapeutic cloning will most likely not be able to do so. Bill C-13 outlaws any sort of procedure of somatic nuclear-cell transfer. The penalty is a maximum of ten years in jail or a half a million dollar fine or both.

How does this strict regime compare to other countries? In the United Kingdom, somatic nuclear-cell transfer is permitted under a licence from the national regulatory body, the Human Fertilization and Embryology Authority, set up in 1990. The United States, like Canada, has no therapeutic cloning legislation, but the Bush administration has said that researchers or institutions who want to receive federal funds are restricted to working with sixty existing lines of stem cells taken from surplus embryos and created before August 9, 2001. However, privately funded researchers in the United States face no such restrictions and some are carrying out somatic nuclear-cell transfers.

The most likely outcome for C-13 is that it will be passed as it is or perhaps in a slightly more restrictive form. It is possible that the Canadian legislation could be amended in Parliament in order that researchers would be limited to working with existing cell lines only. I see little chance that C-13 will move in the other direction, closer to the more open research regimes in the United Kingdom or Sweden or the Netherlands.

Just before the spring 2003 parliamentary recess, C-13 completed what is called the report stage of a bill's passage through the House of Commons. This stage comes after a committee has considered the legislation clause by clause, a process that takes place after the bill is "read" for the second time in the House of Commons. Amendments are proposed by the members of Parliament on the committee and these amendments are voted upon, then the amended bill is sent back to the Commons for the report stage. In general, amendments do not succeed in committee unless they have the support of the majority party in the House of Commons, which will also be the majority party on the committee. But things are less clear-cut with legislation that raises profound ethical and moral issues, and therefore deep passions, as C-13 does.

Many people have misgivings about the use of surplus embryos for research, starting what I shall call the absolutist belief that the embryo is a potential human being from the moment of conception and therefore entitled to the full protection of the law. Yet this fundamental ethical question was not even addressed by the CIHR *ad hoc* working group on stem-cell research. It noted in its final report in January 2002, "While the Working Group respects the diverse viewpoints of respondents on this issue, no attempt was made to articulate an argument regarding the moral status of the embryo as this was not within the mandate of the Working Group" (CIHR, 2002).

Instead, the working group incorporated, without discussion or justification, the moral judgement made earlier in a process closed to the public. That process was the drafting of a policy statement on ethical conduct for human research by what is called the Tri-Council, composed of the three federal granting councils in Canada. The Tri-Council took from 1994 to 1998 to draft its position on the moral status of the embryo and had no meaningful public input. Thus there is this fundamental moral position decided outside the public process altogether and then simply adopted for the CIHR working group's recommendations on stem-cell research.

Nor has there been much discussion in official fora of the next stage of moral objection, the commodification and objectification of an embryo suggested by the widespread use of the word "surplus". A related issue is the use of embryos for curiosity-driven research rather than the life-giving process of assisted reproduction. Finally, many people object to the research on the grounds that scientists should not be playing God by interfering in these matters.

Such a spectrum of belief means that members of Parliament (MPs) are far more likely to hear from opponents of C-13 than from supporters. Most importantly, these opponents warn the MPs that if they do not oppose the bill, they will work to defeat them at the next election. Those are the most horrifying words that any member of Parliament can ever hear, because that person is going to be out leafleting, knocking on doors, writing letters, and eventually driving voters to the polls, to vote for the other candidates.

The government and Health Minister were very concerned that this bill would be amended in committee to even further restrict research access to embryonic stem cells. Their concerns centred not so much on the opposition parties but on somebody in their own party, a Liberal back-bencher named Paul Szabo, who says there is no need for research using embryonic stem cells because adult stem cells will suffice. Other Liberal members less vocal than Paul Szabo are also prepared to vote for restrictive amendments or abstain when C-13 comes to a vote.

Against this high-stakes showdown, the Liberal government made what I think was a strategic blunder. They tried to freeze Paul Szabo out of the parliamentary process. This involves some arcane, but important, parliamentary procedure. The parliamentary whips, a disciplinarian for each party, decide which members sit on various committees. The whip of the Liberal Party refused to appoint Paul Szabo to the committee considering C-13 even though Szabo is one of the most knowledgeable members in this policy area. The committee chair, another liberal, refused to allow Szabo to introduce any amendments to C-13, either directly or through another MP.

The strategic blunder was compounded by a tactical blunder. Because of those strong-arm tactics, when the bill came back to the House of Commons at the report stage Szabo sought to introduce his amendments there. Probably the government's tacticians believed that Szabo would not be able to do this because of a change in the rules of procedure for the House made in 2002. Members had been tying up the Commons by introducing scores of amendments to legislation at the report stage. Therefore, the new rule said no amendments could be introduced at the report stage if there had been a chance to introduce them earlier in the committee stage. But Szabo was denied the chance to introduce his amendments at committee (when they would most likely have been handily defeated); therefore, he had to be allowed to do so at the report stage. Some of the amendments were adopted and now bill C-13 will have third and final reading with more restrictions on stem-cell research than either the federal government or the research community wanted.

The fate of C-13 could get even more bizarre. Health Minister Anne McLellan appears to be counting on the Senate to loosen the research restrictions added by Szabo's amendments. The government is actually contemplating using an unelected body to make changes to legislation approved by an elected body. But the House of Commons must concur in any changes made by the Senate. Members already smarting over the government's bullying tactics are not likely to react kindly to a Senate end-run. Bill C-13 could very well "blow up" all over the place.

I have gone into such excruciating detail for several reasons: (i) to draw attention to the tension between the imperatives of science and ethical concerns in an area of practical genetics; (ii) to underscore that other forces at play may be stronger than either science and ethics, in this case the accommodation of the political system to other people's ethics; and (iii) to point out that the direct political pressure used by people opposed to this piece of legislation is far more effective than the traditional kinds of proponent lobbying such as committee testimony and letter-writing.

Making laws about ethically sensitive forms of research does not have to turn into this sort of horror story. Consider the example of Britain, home to Westminister, the Mother of Parliaments. When Canada was still involved with a Royal Commission in 1990, the government created the Human Fertilization and Embryology Authority. When it became clear that science in this field was moving forward very quickly, the British parliamentary system responded rapidly. An advisory committee report in December 1998 recommended changes to the regulatory regime. In June 1999, the Government of the United Kingdom created an expert panel chaired by the Chief Medical Officer to respond to that report. By April 2000 the panel reported and suggested, among other things, that somatic nuclear-cell transfer be allowed. On December 18, 2000 the House of Commons in the United Kingdom passed the suggested amendments to their legislation. On January 22, 2002 the House of Lords passed the amendments. The amendments came into effect on January 31. In slightly longer than two years, the British managed to update their laws in this contentious area, including a full debate with a free vote in both houses of Parliament.

My conclusion is that once again the Canadian parliamentary process is demonstrating its inability to deal in a timely and an informed fashion with the policy and legal aspects of an emerging scientific issue. But it does not have to be that way.

## REFERENCES

Canadian Institutes of Health Research (CIHR) (2001), *Human Stem Cell Research: Opportunities for Health and Ethical Perspectives.* Ottawa: Supply and Services Canada.

_____ (2002), *Human Pluripotent Stem Cell Research: Recommendations for CIHR-Funded Research.* Ottawa: Supply and Services Canada.

CHAPTER 27

# Ethics and the Need for Independent Scientific Research

## G.H. Reynolds

There seems to be agreement that there is a need for ethics! When individuals use the term "ethics" or discuss the need for "ethical" action, there is usually a presumption that the actor in these cases is someone who finds himself or herself facing a range of choices without seeing a clear, uncomplicated path toward principled, moral action. This emphasis is on the individual. The consideration of ethical choice usually involves an examination of what one person — one prosecutor, one CEO, one public health worker, one policeman, one judge, one scientist — could or should have done in any given circumstance faced. And the analysis of why they did or did not act ethically tends to emphasize their integrity and character as social actors. This type of analysis appears again and again in the media stories about elected officials who took inappropriate campaign contributions, football players who gambled, whistle-blowers who revealed fraudulent accounting schemes, or bad policemen or prosecutors who put innocent people on death row. In part this is because people do terrible things which should be recorded and it sells newspapers. In the area of biomedical research, many reports, papers and books (e.g., Lock, Wells and Farthing, 2001) have addressed the issue of unethical individual conduct in scientific research.

It is harder to talk about ethics as an institutional problem. This is true no matter what type of ethical problem one is dealing with, whether it is the improper exchange of money, conflicts of interest, or racism as a product of institutional practices. It is always more difficult to describe, define, isolate and overcome ethical problems that are fundamentally institutional in nature, and it is easy to understand why. First, institutions are more complicated than individuals. Institutions have come about through a long messy process of evolution, and are the result of an ongoing negotiation of competing interests. Just understanding the way they operate, and their internal and external pressures, takes significant investigation. Secondly, institutions are, by definition, entrenched in the *status-quo* power structures. This means that there is an aversion to changing them significantly, or at least discussing it in public forums, as opposed to tinkering, which seems to be an acceptable method and level of change. Thirdly, institutions, as entities, seem to be neutral and indifferent and, therefore, exempt from the idea that they carry ethical charges or mandates. For example, when the book on IBM and its connections to Nazi Germany was published (Black, 2001), *The Wall Street Journal* excused the company's actions by saying that businesses do business and business is an amoral activity. Of course, this lies in stark contrast to how one thinks about ethical choices made by individuals. Individuals are expected to have the possibility of rising above their own interests, needs, desires, politics and histories in order to act in some way that is abstractly ethical. How can one ask the same thing of an institution?

Consider the case of patented AIDS drugs. Certainly any physician who has taken the Hippocratic oath has a moral obligation to treat a sick person with any drug or therapy at their disposal. Clearly, a physician would be obligated to treat a person with AIDS or HIV positive status with any life-enhancing or life-saving treatments. And such a physician would have to act to treat any opportunistic or secondary infections that come with a compromised immune system. Yet the actions, even the prescriptions, of individual doctors become inseparable from the constraints of their institutional relationships. Doctors do not prescribe existing drugs to millions of patients with AIDS because doing so is not supported by the prevailing institutions that control cost. Drug companies along with governments continue to battle over patent rights and resist the possibility of manufacturing generic versions of those drugs that could save or prolong many lives. It has been estimated that fifty million people around the world will die in days, months or a few years from AIDS unless they are treated with drugs to which they have no access (Kramer, 2003). This is true not only in places like Sub-Saharan Africa, but also in the United States, where 16.2 per cent of the population under 65 years of age were uninsured in 2001 (National Center for Health Statistics, 2003). Even relatively well-off Americans find themselves without insurance by companies who can arbitrarily cap their spending on AIDS-related illnesses, or employers who can terminate sick employees without consequences.

It is this discrepancy between the perceived role of medicine and the failure of the delivery of medical services, at such an enormous cost in human suffering, that has marked this issue as an ethical crisis. The battle being waged around the world by activists for treatment access is rapidly becoming one of the most symbolic catastrophes of institutional ethics in our time.

But what about examples of ethical compromise which may not have such stark consequences? What can we expect from individuals within institutions, and how can one develop a framework for talking about ethics that acknowledges the position of the person within an institutional framework while insisting upon individual responsibility? In some institutions, individuals face a range of choices without seeing a clear, uncomplicated path toward principled, moral action.

Although any number of institutional relationships might be examined in this way, I want to further examine the network of scientific research that has come to be called the "military-industrial-academic complex". In an historical period characterized by the acceleration of information production and delivery, one has seen the convergence of forces that produce information. Like military-industrial complex or prison-industrial complex, the term military-industrial-academic complex is a way to describe and highlight the increasing interdependence of one type of institution with another. In terms of the production of science and scientific research, the goals and interests of academic, military and industrial institutions have begun to coincide. To think about this, it is helpful to consider why each institution conducts scientific research, how such work is funded, how the outcomes are evaluated, disputed and utilized, and how much room there is for individuals inside and outside the institutions to evaluate the results (Reppy, 1999).

"Instrumental" science is a term for research that has the goal of creating marketable products, and understandably, such applied scientific endeavors are most often associated with corporate support. Scientific research that seeks to advance scientific knowledge in a more general, abstract sense is often referred to as "non-instrumental" research. Although there are certainly overlaps between these areas, as non-instrumental research lays the groundwork for future applied work, and applied work provides unexpected insight into all kinds of scientific questions, these terms are helpful in distinguishing the intended aims of a particular scientific inquiry. Non-instrumental research is carried out by parties who are disinterested in the findings. The results are made available for public use. However, the goal of corporate research is proprietary, which means it does not benefit the corporation to share scientific discoveries. Furthermore, proprietary interests in the pursuit of knowledge raise concerns about conflicts of interest. The increasing tendency for scientific research to take place at research universities, utilizing corporate funding generates an even more difficult question that is ontological in nature and addresses the question of what types of science are produced at all (Ho, 2001).

It may be helpful to think about science as something that is "produced" like a product. In other words, we produce certain understandings of the world based on what questions are asked and what is studied. No matter what types of experiments are pursued, our model of the world changes with the results. And this is true whether the project is nuclear waste, plants of the tropical rainforest, the anger gene, antiviral drugs or artificial sweeteners. That is why the question of what scientific research one does speaks to a broader question of what one wants the world to become. There is a lot at stake in that question.

But the form of ethical compromise is impossible to visualize if the focus is only on the actions of individuals. A good example of this is cancer research, a field with many excellent scientists in pursuit of breakthroughs and discoveries. Studies have shown that many cancers have environmental causes or influences. However, research and prevention in this area are under-funded. Further, much cancer research directed toward prevention seeks to identify putative genes that predispose people to cancer, rather than known (or suspected) environmental causes. Health effects, like ecological effects, remain vastly understudied due to the influence of the chemical industry in universities and in government. In order to think about "good science" one has to take a step back from the actions that take place in the laboratory, and think about why the laboratory is there to begin with, who put it there, and what is not there.

As public universities find themselves facing tighter and tighter budgets, one can expect their dependence on instrumental funding sources to grow accordingly. Since the *Bayh-Dole Act* of 1980 in the United States, which allows universities to take patents on the results of federally funded research, some academic institutions have become businesses in their own right, seeking to commercialize research discoveries rather than preserve their status as independent, disinterested scholars. Although such patents may help universities continue to fund their non-instrumental research, it also raises questions. Do academic institutions feel the need to emphasize instrumental research knowing that they can gain financially from the results? Does non-instrumental research become more difficult to justify financially under these pressures?

Much of federally financed research contributes directly to new drugs, treatments and discoveries that corporations ultimately utilize in new patents. Part of the explanation that drug companies give for the tremendous price of drugs is the need to fold in the cost of past and future research and development, something that has been subsidized by academic institutions and government.

What has resulted from the military-industrial-academic complex, is the convergence of institutional pressures that, I believe, will mean the scientific community may well lose a large degree of its independence, its ability to pursue knowledge for knowledge's sake. I see this lack of independence as an issue of ethics because it involves the decisions and actions of institutions and individuals in possession of an enormous amount of power, power that is not subject to democratic control.

There is a need for a strong and independent scientific community that is engaged in the advancement of knowledge and in the creation of a better world, not only for humans but for all life on Earth. There is the involvement of the Union of Concerned Scientists on issues ranging from nuclear arms control to concerns about genetically modified foods. As sixteen hundred scientists stated in their "Warning to Humanity" after the 1992 Earth Summit in Rio de Janeiro, humanity is on a collision course with the natural world, the global ecosystem is being affected by humans unlike any other organism in our planet's history. The Union of Concerned Scientists calls for a new attitude toward discharging our responsibility for caring for ourselves and for the earth, and a new ethic (Union of Concerned Scientists, 1992). These examples show scientists stepping out of their institutional affiliations and creating issue groups which can use their clout and access to information to try to influence institutional structures and public policies. This is an exciting solution to the problem of the individuals who find themselves without a clear path for ethical action within their institutional roles. But it is important to evaluate these approaches and ask what other strategies there may be.

How can scientists acknowledge their unique position as guardians of human health and as custodians of the natural world? They should not go on creating new technologies without accepting responsibility for their implementation and control, or fulfilling their roles in institutions that increasingly have interests that can compromise a sound and ethical pursuit of scientific knowledge. A new ethic would prevent the scientific community from relinquishing this duty to corporate or governmental interests which are incapable or unwilling to understand their properties or potential. If the scientific community were to have a Hippocratic oath of its own, a code of ethics that held individual scientists accountable to those "under their care" (so to speak), perhaps it would be easier for us to recognize the power that scientists hold in the modern world — a power of life and death infinitely greater than Hippocrates could have imagined — and perhaps we would have greater expectations of the scientific community to work for the public good.

## NOTE

The presentation and paper represent the personal views of the author, and do not necessarily reflect the views of any government agency.

## REFERENCES

Black, E. (2001), *IBM and the Holocaust: The Strategic Alliance between Nazi Germany and America's Most Powerful Corporation*. New York: Crown Publishers.

Ho, M.-W. (2001), "Why Biotech Patents are Patently Absurd", *The Institute of Science in Society*. At <http://www.i-sis.org.uk/trips2.php>.

Kramer, L. (2003), "The Plague We Can't Escape", *New York Times*, March 17.

Lock, S., Wells, F. and Farthing, M., eds. (2001), *Fraud and Misconduct in Biomedical Research*, 3d ed. London: British Medical Association.

National Center for Health Statistics (2003), *Health, United States 2003*. Hyattsville, MD: National Center for Health Statistics.

Reppy, J., ed. (1999), *Secrecy and Knowledge Production*. Occasional Paper No. 23. Ithaca, NY: Peace Studies Program, Cornell University.

Union of Concerned Scientists (1992), "World Scientists' Warning to Humanity". At <http://www.environment.harvard.edu/religion/publications/statements/union.html>.

# PART XI

## DISCUSSION AND CONCLUSIONS

CHAPTER 28

# End Notes

---

## F.H. Berkshire

Instead of being largely confined to trying to make some sense of my own designated theme and thoughts, it has been a new experience for me to try to react in a studied way to those of others, rather than on an *ad hoc* basis. There have been a lot of challenging questions raised and debated here — with no easy answers.

The questions are, in no particular order:

- What balance should be struck between self-regulation and external regulation of individual professions?
- How can academic freedom and political/commercial influence co-exist happily?
- Where should the line be drawn between individual/collective rights and duties/responsibilities?
- Should we need to regulate for what should be common decency?
- How can we deal with the influence of terrorism and global crime?
- In dangerous times how much freedom and privacy can we afford?
- In academic and public matters, where is the line separating delusion and misconduct?
- With public relations and the embracing of the media, must we take the rough with the smooth?
- How strongly can we seek to correlate justice with truth, particularly in a global corporate environment?
- Can justice be made more accessible?

All of these questions reside in an increasingly complex and dangerous world, in which we cannot assume that law and order will triumph in the end.

In the *Opening Session,* we heard, by way of a tale of water quality, that regulation is normally introduced as a reaction to disaster. However, it seems to me that such regulation, rather than a reliance on professional integrity, quite often leads to a worsening of overall standards, because regulation can only be done at a level that is acceptable to all (and not only specifically commercial) interests.

In *Science in the Courts* the matter of expert opinion was raised, together with who is to decide which such opinion to consult and with what weight. In a gladiatorial legal contest the truth may very often be a casualty in a duel between competing experts. An independent court-appointed expert is a rarity.

I confess that my personal experience of this is rather limited. I do remember receiving a personal letter which began:

> *I, like my colleague, am serving a life sentence for murder. In his case there has been a miscarriage of justice....*

This turned out to be a case of "murder by Mark 10 Jaguar" and my dynamics expertise was being consulted. Let us just say I answered this letter *very* carefully. What struck a chord here at this meeting was Professor Merry's remark that "Science deals with the world as it is, but law deals with a man-made version of the world as it ought to be".

In *Government and Science,* it was stated that government needs information rather than advice, but that this needs to be independently given. However, there seems to me to be something of a language problem in the practicalities of this and I found myself conjugating:

> I have measured opinions,
> You are arrogant,
> We hold the keys to knowledge,
> They are ignorant philistines.

In *Science, Public Opinion and the Media,* there seemed to be at least an uneasy truce. The need for mutual trust was emphasized and scientists seemed to accept the accusation of being their own worst enemy in dealing with the media. Ms. Park's video film example debunking the moon landings seemed not so much anti-science as bad science and apparently pro-conspiracy. This brought home the point that the scientific community has an obligation to take on a responsible policing role — inaction is more painful than action here, at least in the medium to long term.

In *Research, Security and Secrecy*, Dr. Howard, with his military background, urged scientists to communicate, according to the intended audience. Whilst the SOCO (Single, Overriding Communication Objective) is probably still, in my view, "the medium is not the message, the message is the message", the medium is a vital adjunct. Dr. Howard's notion of lobbying as game theory, survival of the fittest, appeals to my competitive nature. However, since funding comes from a finite budget, a finite *science* budget, money won is inevitably at other projects' loss and they may well be more deserving of support.

In *Ethics*, I was impressed by the idea of the university as a scholars' guild as part of self-regulation of the professions, although this seems to be eroding rapidly. From Professor Wolpert we heard that "science is value-free" and I think I know what he means. But please do not put it to government this way; we have enough trouble with "fitness for the world of work" and "technological spin-off requirements" as it is. However, his important afterthought about "rationing of medical resources" is surely one for a future conference.

In *National Disasters, Terrorism and Public Safety,* one idea not well addressed is that while we are used to a free and frank exchange there is a certain resentment of aspects of commercial confidentiality. Education is an international commodity. How are we to change our processes with regard to international groups of students, academics and researchers, especially when many come from countries that might not remain friendly? In any event, friendship is not always mathematically transitive.

In *Crime and Morality*, we heard from Dr. Del Buono about the matter of duties *versus* rights and from Professor Hand about the political and public implications of the collection of, and collation processes for, crime data.

Professor McKee's theme was scientific delusion and misconduct. This raised questions of their real level of occurrence and quite how much damage is caused when they are detected (or undetected). Indeed it can be asked quite seriously whether they can ever be a good thing.

In the final section, *Genes, Ethics and Science*, Peter Calamai gave a graphic illustration of the delights of parliamentary procedures, in allowing interested parties to sideline reports and delay regulation and legislation.

In this regard, I found it a somewhat unexpected pleasure to hear the words drive and urgency used in connection with activity at the "Mother of Parliaments" at Westminster — things must be worse elsewhere than I had thought.

In conclusion, my main concern remains in the wider influence that these conferences, and the ideas discussed, might have. Many scientists may not feel they do, or should, care, other than in narrow personal terms, and those who do may well feel that they cannot make a difference.

In this regard, the comedian Fred Allen once mused "A conference is a gathering of important people who singly can do nothing, but together can decide that nothing can be done". Let us negate this definition and fan the flames of the ideas sparked here at Herstmonceux Castle.

CHAPTER 29

# Science, Ethics and the Law: Concluding Observations

## V.M. Del Buono

A successful conference always produces more questions than answers. This one is no exception, and these are the questions that I came away with.

First, how does science deal with ambiguity? Not the ambiguity of the unknown in the realm of physical matter but rather the ambiguity that is grounded in public values, feelings and beliefs.

Secondly, how do different disciplines think about causality? Discovering what causes events to happen or results to occur is a question that vexes anyone who seeks to achieve a proscribed outcome. In science, many controlled experiments seek first to isolate and then to test a cause and effect relationship, within a reality in which multiple causes invariably interact to produce multiple effects. In the formulation of public policy, on the other hand, it is quite rare that one has an opportunity to rigorously test for a single cause and effect relationship. Where we are not able to (and in public policy this is almost always the case), what degree of authority are we willing to ascribe to our assumptions or conclusions about causation?

In retrospect, I would have wanted us to explore more fully the role that prediction, and specifically risk prediction, plays in both science and public policy. Most scientists, perhaps because they are more sensible than the rest of us, are generally reluctant to make predictions. Scientists formulate theories and hypotheses to be tested against fact. But prediction is better left to soothsayers and the like. Public policy, which is always purposeful on the other hand, seems to demand constant calculation and recalculation in which one is always trying to figure out whether an act or series of acts will produce a desired outcome. Needless to say, it is extremely difficult to "get it right" when circumstances are ever shifting and subjective perceptions are such an important factor. Statisticians have perfected the science of polling so that we can accurately capture and describe almost every aspect of public attitudes and opinion. However, the science of accessing those attitudes or getting opinions to change is far less certain.

Thirdly, some participants have commented that we are becoming a society that seems to be obsessed with the attribution of blame. Why has there been the growth of a "blame society"? I thought it quite odd that a conference of scientists would not express strong doubts about the limits of a blame society because of the premise that underlies the notion: that everything is based on human agency and accordingly human beings can be held responsible for everything that occurs. Is this a scientifically observable phenomenon? What has happened to nature? Is the notion of an act of God completely passé? If a loss or injury occurs, which was unexpected, must there always be someone to blame? What for? Having miscalculated the risks? Rules for the attribution of responsibility for actions and omissions with a view to punishment are at the core of criminal law. One of the most fundamental is that a person needs to have *mens rea*, a certain state of mind, a certain admixture of awareness, knowledge and, often, will to be criminally responsible for certain acts or, in the case of criminal omissions, outcomes.

Fourthly, I was struck by the difference that was drawn by one of the participants between an error and a violation. Is this simply another way of approaching the discussion of whether human agency is the organizing principle of our world? Does the dichotomy "error/violation" presume that there is at all times a right answer?

My final question is why this conference of distinguished scientists and statisticians did not explore one of the most pressing public issues involving "Statistics, Science and Public Policy" and "Science, Ethics and the Law" – the use of profiling in many aspects of our everyday life. Profiling involves the use of certain information and statistical methods to assess or predict the probability of a specific individual possessing certain attributes, attitudes or engaging in a particular conduct. The debates about profiling subsume many of the other questions that I have mentioned so far.

Profiling is used extensively in marketing as well as in law enforcement to maximize the impact of limited resources by calculating whom to target as most likely to buy or, in the case of the law enforcement, to transgress. As we know, it is currently being used to decide which taxpayers to target for audits in order to maximize recovery of unpaid taxes from delinquents or evaders. Most of us, with the possible exception of those who have been targeted themselves, would applaud the use of profiling for such a worthwhile public purpose. Profiling is also being used to sift through millions of transactions to try to identify those that may constitute money laundering. Following the terrorism of 9/11, the use of profiling in airport immigration queues and other border crossings has increased dramatically.

The use of racial profiling in policing is perhaps the most highly contested issue this conference could have dealt with. It has become so sensitive that even the mere mention of it is taboo. There have been even occasions where a skittish public official has denied its existence in the face of overwhelming evidence to the contrary. It is a flash point for race relations in many cities in Europe and North America. Racial profiling is used by law-enforcement agencies to determine individual guilt based only on race, ethnicity or national origin. Several years ago, an End Racial Profiling Act of 2001 was introduced in the U.S. House of Representatives, but was not passed.

The debate around racial profiling is one in which scientists and especially statisticians have a very important role to play. There is a considerable amount of fear, prejudice and emotion around the issue of its use. Is there any scientific validity to the assumptions about the proclivity to commit crime of certain racial, ethnic or national groups that underlie racial profiling? If there is none, then the scientific and statistical community should clearly say so. If the conclusion is that there is or may be, then scientific opinion should weigh in.

Would not a conference on "Science, Ethics and the Law" with panels that dealt with government, public opinion, the media, research, security, secrecy, ethics, terrorism, public safety, crime, morality, truth and justice not have been a marvelous forum for just such a discussion?

# APPENDIX

# CONFERENCE ON STATISTICS, SCIENCE AND PUBLIC POLICY

## 23-26 APRIL 2003 SCIENCE, ETHICS AND THE LAW

**Queen's University International Study Centre    Herstmonceux Castle    Hailsham, U.K.**

# PROGRAMME

# WEDNESDAY 23 APRIL

**Reception**
17.00 – 18.00

**Dinner**
18.00 – 19.00

**Opening Session**
19.30 – 21.00
19.30 Introduction
19.45 M.S. McQuigge *Owen Sound, Canada*
20.30 Discussion

# THURSDAY 24 APRIL

A. **Science in the Courts**
   8.30 - 10.15
   8.30 Introduction
   8.35 W.B. Allen *Michigan State University*
   8.50 R.H. McKercher *McKercher, McKercher and*
   *Whitmore, Saskatoon*
   9.05 A.F. Merry *University of Auckland*
   9.20 Discussion

B. **Government and Science**
   10.45 - 12.30
   10.45 Introduction
   10.50 J.C. Bailar *University of Chicago*
   11.05 D.H. Irvine *Picker Institute, Europe*
   11.20 M.S. McQuigge *Owen Sound, Canada*
   11.35 Discussion

C. **Science, Public Opinion and the Media**
   14.00 - 15.45
   14.00 Introduction
   14.05 T. Jefferson *Cochrane Vaccines Field*
   14.20 P. Kavanagh *Canadian Broadcasting Corporation*
   14.35 P. Park *Discovery Channel, Canada*
   14.55 Discussion

D. **Research, Security and Secrecy**
   16.15 - 18.00
   16.15 Introduction
   16.20 E.B. Andersen *University of Copenhagen*
   16.35 R.J. Howard *Harvard University/Key3 Media*
   16.50 Discussion

**Dinner**
18.00 – 19.00

**Concert**
19.30
Gerald Finley *baritone*
Julius Drake *pianist*

**Refreshments**

# FRIDAY 25 APRIL

### E. Ethics
**8.30 - 10.15**
8.30 Introduction
8.35 H.B. Dinsdale *Queen's University*
8.50 A.F. Merry *University of Auckland*
9.05 L. Wolpert *University College London*
9.20 Discussion

### F. Natural Disasters, Terrorism and Public Safety
**10.45 - 12.30**
10.45 Introduction
10.50 B. Farbey *University College London*
11.05 R.T. Haworth *Natural Resources Canada*
11.20 R.J. Howard *Harvard University/Key3 Media*
11.35 Discussion

### G. Crime and Morality
**14.00 - 15.45**
14.00 Introduction
14.05 V.M. Del Buono *British Council, Nigeria*
14.20 D.J. Hand *Imperial College of Science, Technology and Medicine*
14.35 J.S.C. McKee *University of Manitoba*
14.50 Discussion

### H. Truth *versus* Justice – Panel Discussion
**16.15 - 18.00**
*Chairman* P. Milliken *Canadian House of Commons*
P. Calamai *Toronto Star*
R.H. McKercher *McKercher, McKercher and Whitmore, Saskatoon*
J.M. Spence *Superior Court of Justice of Ontario*

### Banquet
**19.00 - 21.00**
20.00 J.S.C. McKee *University of Manitoba*

# SATURDAY 26 APRIL

### I. Genes, Ethics and Science
**8.30 - 10.15**
8.30 Introduction
8.35 P. Calamai *Toronto Star*
8.50 G.H. Reynolds *Centers for Disease Control and Prevention*
9.05 To be announced
9.20 Discussion

### J. Discussion and Conclusions
**10.45 - 12.30**
10.45 Introduction
10.50 F. H. Berkshire *Imperial College of Science, Technology and Medicine*
11.05 V.M. Del Buono *British Council, Nigeria*
11.20 T. Jefferson *Cochrane Vaccines Field*
11.35 Discussion

*We gratefully acknowledge the following benefactors whose generosity has made this Conference possible:*

Berry Brothers & Rudd Ltd.

Camera Kingston

Campus Bookstore, Queen's University

Canada Foundation for Innovation

Environment Canada

Galerie d'Art Vincent, Château Laurier, Ottawa

National Research Council of Canada

Natural Resources Canada

Natural Sciences and Engineering Research Council of Canada

Queen's University

Many anonymous donors are also gratefully thanked.

Cover photograph courtesy of H.B. Dinsdale

# CONFERENCE on STATISTICS, SCIENCE and PUBLIC POLICY

## 23-26 APRIL 2003 SCIENCE, ETHICS AND THE LAW

**Queen's University International Study Centre   Herstmonceux Castle   Hailsham, U.K.**

## LIST OF PARTICIPANTS

C.M. Allen *Michigan State University*

W.B. Allen *Michigan State University*

E.B. Andersen *University of Copenhagen*

D.F. Andrews *University of Toronto*

J.C. Bailar *University of Chicago*

F.H. Berkshire *Imperial College of Science, Technology and Medicine*

P. Calamai *Toronto Star*

M. Cappe *Canadian High Commission, U.K.*

V.M. Del Buono *British Council, Nigeria*

E. Didier *Ottawa, Canada*

H.B. Dinsdale *Kingston General Hospital and Queen's University*

S.R. Esterby *Okanagan University College*

B. Farbey *University College London*

T.G. Flynn *Queen's University*

D.H. Foster *University of Manchester Institute of Science and Technology*

O. Güvenen *Bilkent University*

D.J. Hand *Imperial College of Science, Technology and Medicine*

R.T. Haworth *Natural Resources Canada*

A.M. Herzberg *Queen's University*

R.J. Howard *Harvard University/Key3 Media*

K.U. Ingold *National Research Council of Canada*

D.H. Irvine *Picker Institute, Europe*

T. Jefferson *Cochrane Vaccines Field*

R.M. Kassen *University of Oxford*

P. Kavanagh *Canadian Broadcasting Corporation*

J.S.C. McKee *University of Manitoba*

M.L. McKercher *University of Saskatchewan*

R.H. McKercher *McKercher, McKercher and Whitmore, Saskatoon*

M.S. McQuigge *Owen Sound, Canada*

A.F. Merry *University of Auckland*

P. Milliken *Canadian House of Commons*

L.T. Nau *Natural Sciences and Engineering Research Council of Canada*

R.W. Oldford *University of Waterloo*

P. Park *Discovery Channel, Canada*

G.H. Reynolds *Centers for Disease Control and Prevention*

J.M. Spence *Superior Court of Justice of Ontario*

R.J. Tomkins *University of Regina*

D.H. Turpin *University of Victoria*

L. Wolpert *University College London*

# GERALD FINLEY
*Baritone*

# JULIUS DRAKE
*Pianist*

## Programme for recital at Herstmonceux Castle
## 24 April 2003

**WOLFGANG AMADEUS MOZART**
*Papageno's aria Der Vogelfänger from the Magic Flute*
*Serenade from Don Giovanni*
*Figaro aria from the Marriage of Figaro*

**LUDWIG VAN BEETHOVEN**
*Selbstgespräch (Ich, der mit flatterndem Sinn)*
*Wonne der Wehmut,* from op. 83
*Adelaide,* op. 46 ( ca. 1794-5)
*In questa tomba oscura*
*Der Kuss,* op.128 (1822)
*An die ferne Geliebte,* op. 98

*INTERMISSION*

**JOHANNES BRAHMS – HÖLTY SETTINGS**
*Minnelied,* op. 71 no. 5
*An die Nachtigall,* op. 46 no.4
*Der Kuss,* op. 19 no.12
*Die Mainacht,* op. 43 no.2
*An ein Veilchen,* op. 49 no.2

**RALPH VAUGHAN WILLIAMS** *Whither must I wander*

**ARR. BENJAMIN BRITTEN** *The Ash Grove*

**MARK ANTHONY TURNAGE** *The Silver Tassie*

**WOLSELEY CHARLES** *The Green Eyed Dragon*